Preserves, Pickles & Cures

Preserves, Pickles & Cures

THANE PRINCE

PHOTOGRAPHY BY DIANA MILLER
ILLUSTRATIONS BY SUE ROBSON

PAVILION

For Maisie MacIntyre, with love.

This edition published in the United Kingdom
in 2015 by Pavilion
1 Gower Street, London WC1E 6HD

Text © Thane Prince, 2011
Design and layout © Pavilion Books, 2011
Photography © Pavilion Books, 2011

ISBN: 978-1-91049-6-03-9

A CIP catalogue record for this book is available
from the British Library.

10 9 8 7 6 5 4 3 2 1

Colour reproduction by Mission Productions,
Hong Kong
Printed and bound by Craft Print Ltd, Singapore

www.pavilionbooks.com

Commissioning Editor:
Emily Preece-Morrison
Layout:
Louise Leffler
Photography:
Diana Miller
Food Styling:
Joy Skipper
Prop Styling:
Wei Tang
Editor:
Susan Fleming
Illustrations:
Sue Robson
Indexer:
Patricia Hymans

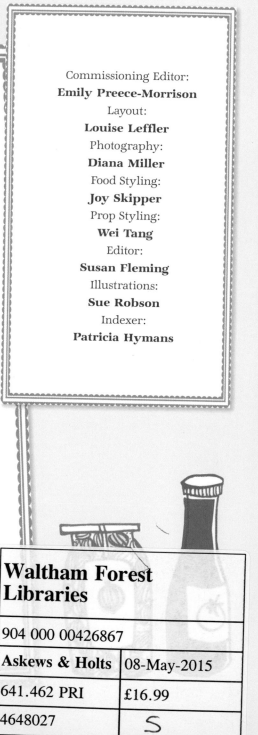

Contents

INTRODUCTION

There is something quite remarkable about the world of larders. Billy Bunter loved larders, full of treats for high teas; Huckleberry Finn raided his Aunt Polly's larder and had to paint her fence in recompense. The very word conjures up in one's mind a place of plenty and delight. That this is still true is quite remarkable in this age of 24-hour shopping, with markets, supermarkets, specialist cheese shops and on-line grocery orders.

We are, wherever we live, seldom more than a few miles or a click of the mouse from any number of cooking essentials or delicious treats, so why the nostalgia for a small, shelved room situated on the north side of the house, filled with strange often unmarked jars, the odd musty smell of ripened fruit and a distinct chill in the air?

I think our yearning for larders, and it is not uncommon for this to be the deciding factor when choosing a new home, is due to a longing for certainty in our wonderful but frantic world. Everything is transient, available and allowed. How nice then to remember and recreate a space where things are stored, left to mature, kept for special occasions and emergencies, a place where life moves slowly and with purpose. Where thrift and economy go hand-in-hand with the skill of a good housekeeper.

It is no coincidence that the rise in larders accompanies the quest for allotments, and a yearning to grow one's own food, keep a few chickens, and even a return to the idea of a cottage pig. The rediscovery of the flavours of home-made, home-grown food has brought about a change in the way we regard our store-cupboards for just as home-cooked food is delicious, home-preserved food can also be wonderful. And what better time to take up this mantle, for now home-preserving accompanies home cooking, and all with splendid produce. Not for us the simple need to fill our larders with all that the garden produced, no matter the quality, in order to survive the winter, but the luxury of choice in what we preserve.

Only the best and ripest fruit and vegetables, only the most carefully raised cured meats, the artisan cheeses, perhaps those special tins of fish bought when in Spain, spice mixes from North Africa, in all a room stocked with undreamt of delights. So although the allure of the pantry is now more about the exotic than the staple, those staples must be considered too. And even with staples there are good choices to be made. There has been, over recent years, a heartening rise in the number of people bringing traditional food production methods back into use, and also bringing those methods up to date. Mills grind local grains into flours and seeds into oils, vinegar is made from local apples, and a British balsamic-type cider vinegar is being made in Suffolk. Any number of small producers make artisan cordials, pickles, jams and mustards. Stocking your larder could then be a simple matter of buying well, as you visit farmers' markets and delicatessens. But to simply stock your larder with bought produce is to miss the very real sense of satisfaction that comes from making your own.

For cooking your own preserves, salting and curing your own meats, and bottling your own cordials to stock your larder shelves, is well within the reach of even the beginner in the kitchen.

The recipes in this book have been tested with that very much in mind, and if a few simple rules are followed, you will amaze and impress your family and friends.

The Perfect Larder or Pantry

If you are lucky enough to have found a house with a pantry or larder still intact – a great many were knocked out at the advent of good refrigeration – then you are blessed indeed. I am assured that these days a larder can add thousand pounds' worth of value to homes as more and more people recognise their merit.

The essence of a larder is a north-facing room, and it is best with two outside walls. The ventilation should be through airbricks, one top and one bottom, both covered with fine, fly-proof mesh. The main shelving can be of wood but there must always be a marble slab. This slab is the very soul of the larder: as I write, I see a ham covered with cheesecloth, a hunk of Stilton or Cheddar, some bottles of squash and a bread crock sitting on top of the slab.

The larder should be easy to clean and as the focus is on cold, dry storage, a slate or stone floor is best. No natural light is needed; in fact dark cold is what you most require. Baskets for potatoes and root vegetables can be arranged under the marble slab and dried herbs and salamis can be hung from ceiling hooks.

A pantry is what many more of us can achieve. The definition of pantry is a small room, more likely a cupboard, with the capacity to store food. Many modern kitchens have wonderful pantry cupboards built into them complete with granite slab to recreate the feel of a larder. Whilst these are often very beautiful additions to the kitchen, they do not possess the main feature of a larder, which is its low temperature. A cupboard in a centrally heated room, no matter how well designed, whilst accommodating many foodstuffs, will have to be accompanied by a larger fridge than that needed if you have a cold room or larder.

You can of course be inventive in your search for a larder. I have a friend who uses her cellar: it's dark and cold though a little damp, so again you must take care what you store there. If the cellar can be well ventilated it can be a perfect place to store root vegetables, apples, pears and whole hams etc. Out-houses can be perfect, but they still need the essential qualities of cold, dry and dark. You must also make sure they are bug-free and that there is no access for rodents!

A Return to Traditional Skills

Along with the loss of our larders came the loss of many of the essential skills needed to prepare and preserve food. It was once a source of great pride to any housewife that her larder was well ordered, well stocked and a credit to her home-making skills.

Old cookery books, for instance, place great store on thrift. The need to husband and preserve all remnants of fat is particularly fascinating. Fat make an excellent vehicle for storing preserved foods, and in history fats were most careful rendered and stored. This appreciation of fat is somewhat agin the modern way, which can often seem to be looking at those two stalwarts of the traditional larder – fat and salt – as public enemies. It is a source of some amusement to me that at a time when we lived on highly salted, fatty foods we had much less obesity than now when the horror of low-fat foods congests our fridges.

The ability to source, cook and store food for the family was once essential knowledge handed from mother to daughter. Jane Austen writes of the Bennet girls gathering and drying herbs, Tudor housewives guarded their receipts carefully, and a generation of cookery teachers tried to inspire a love of food and basic skills to often uninterested girls. I remember my own cookery lessons with dismay. The food seemed dull and the rules excessive. I'm afraid I didn't shine...

Now, though, cooking is exciting, food colourful and packed with flavour and the emphasis is on joy rather than drudgery. And the kitchen is open to all-comers for gender is no longer an issue. Cookery schools are flourishing as people with a genuine interest in food try and catch up on skills that have been lost to them.

Baking bread, making pastry, pickling vegetables, salting fish, rendering fats and all manner of simple but pleasing accomplishments that in themselves give satisfaction. This book will, I hope, inspire you to try new ideas, become confident in your skills, stock your larder shelves with glorious preserves, fill your cake tins with gingerbread and flapjacks, and so give you the sense of satisfaction that comes from a job well done.

CHEESE AND DAIRY

Introduction

Milk lies at the heart of everything to do with cheese and dairy. It is our earliest food and one of the most valuable to our health. A glass of milk contains proteins, vitamins and calcium, and while the fat content varies over the spectrum of grades of milk, there is little reason why we shouldn't drink and enjoy milk every day.

I've always thought that one of the factors that mitigates against milk is that we are taught from an early age that drinking a glass a day is good for you. A disaster in terms of PR, as who wants to do something just because it's good for you? Many people avoid milk as they feel it is full of fat, but, as you will see below, this is a misconception.

One interesting observation is that, due to the rise of coffee shops on the high street selling vats of cappuccino, milk intake has increased among young women…

Milk

If my local supermarket is a guide, we are not only drinking a lot of cow's milk but also a wide variety of other milks, amongst them goat's and ewe's or sheep's milk. I have specified which type of milk to use in the recipes in this chapter. All varieties of milk are best stored in the fridge.

Cow's Milk

Full-fat (whole) cow's milk has 4% fat, yes, just 4%. If you ask a random group of people, they never guess that the fat content is so low. While the fat carries many of milk's essential vitamins, if you drop the fat content to 2%, which is known as semi-skimmed, you will still have significant quantities of vitamin A in your diet. The calcium levels in milk do not vary greatly between the different grades. Low-fat milk has 1% fat, and skimmed milk a negligible quantity. These lower-fat milks obviously contain less fat-soluble vitamins but much the same amount of calcium.

Fresh milk in the UK is sold pasteurized – heat-treated to destroy bacteria. This treatment is carried out at 72ºC/161ºF, and should not be confused with UHT milk, which is heat-treated to 135ºC/275ºF to extend its shelf life. UHT milk can be stored unopened for six months, but once opened should be treated as fresh milk. Raw milk is sold on a small number of farms, but is not commonly available.

Goat's Milk

This milk is becoming widely available as people search for alternatives to cow's milk, believing erroneously that these milks are easier to digest. It should be remembered that goat's milk, along with all animal milk, does contain lactose and so is not suitable for those who are lactose intolerant. It's also not recommended as a cow's milk substitute for babies, as it is low in folic acid and vitamin B12.

Goat's milk is high in calcium, and makes good yoghurts.

Ewe's Milk

This is not widely available in milk form, but is the base for real Greek yoghurt. It is a rich creamy milk that is made into one of my favourite cheeses, Roquefort.

Cheese-making

At one time, milk was only available in its fresh form in spring and summer after the cows had calved. Once the herd was in calf again, the supply literally dried up. Milk was a very good source of protein and fat, the importance of which I've discussed above. To preserve these nutrients in a product that can spoil in 24 hours then becomes crucial.

That milk sours and becomes unpleasant quickly, more so in the days before we understood the role bacteria played in this process, meant it was imperative to try and find a way to process milk to extend its useful life.

It's hard to be exact about the beginnings of cheese-making, where it started, and how. I feel it's likely that there were many countries that invented cheese-making at much the same time.

There are many ways of making cheese that give the wonderful selection that we can buy in our markets and cheese shops. Every dairy guards their process with care. The addition of salt, herbs, coating with ash, the inoculation of blueing bacteria, maturing in caves – there are thousands of different processes that cheese can go through in order to create its many varied and differing flavours.

The source of the milk, too, has a profound effect on the flavour, with goat's and ewe's milk cheeses tasting completely different to cow's milk cheeses. And where the animal grazes also influences the flavour of the cheese, with summer milk cheeses being more fragrant and with a somewhat higher fat content than those made from winter milk. Cows are milked twice a day, and as there is even a difference between the evening and morning milk, milks from the two milkings are usually combined to make cheese.

Cheese is made by mixing rennet into whole milk and collecting the curd that forms. Quite how it was discovered that rennet, an enzyme found in the stomach of calves, caused the curds to separate from the whey takes a bit of imagination. I go with the theory that

sees milk being stored in a bag made from the stomach of a young animal which, when opened, was found to have separated into curds and whey. All young milk-fed animals have rennet in their stomach, but calf's rennet was most commonly used. The fourth stomach of the calf was cleaned and the stomach wall scraped for the rennet, which was then mixed into the milk. To ensure a continuous supply of rennet the stomach was dried and stored until needed when small pieces were reconstituted and the process continued as above.

Acid also curdles milk and I've used lemon juice to make my paneer cheese on page 17.

Rennet can be bought in tablet, powder or liquid form (and is now available commercially in vegetarian form). I use liquid rennet to make junket, a wonderfully elegant milk dessert which has been made in Britain since the Middle Ages. It is thought Miss Muffet was eating junket when frightened by the spider in the nursery rhyme, for, as you eat junket, the curds separate from the whey. To make junket I follow the instructions given on the rennet bottle, flavouring it with a few drops of rosewater and adding one drop of cochineal to tint the pudding a gentle pink.

In cheese-making, once the curd has been separated from the whey, it can be processed in a dozen ways. At its simplest, the curd is put into a mould and the whey will gradually drip away – soft fresh cheeses like the ones in this chapter are the result. Other curds are cut sparingly to help the whey drain away; this is used for soft cheeses (Brie and Camembert curds, for instance, are hardly cut at all). Harder cheeses are made from curd that has been cut much more substantially, thereby releasing a great deal more liquid. Cheeses like Cheddar are made by a process known as 'cheddaring', in which the curd is cut minimally into blocks which are piled on top of each other – this allows the whey to be expelled, while retaining the smoothness of the curd. It is this that gives the cheese its distinct texture.

The whey that drains from the curd still contains proteins which can be used to make what are known as whey cheeses. Heating this whey causes the proteins to coagulate and fuse together. Whey cheeses include Norwegian *gjetost* and Italian ricotta. The whey is used also as animal feed, as it is very nutritious. There is a great synergy between cheese-making and pig-farming, as pigs love whey. So it is no coincidence that Parma ham and Parmesan cheese come from the same region.

After the initial separation of curd and whey, cheeses are variously salted, pressed and ripened. At home this is difficult, so the recipes I have given are for fresh cheeses only.

Cheese is best served at room temperature when its flavour shows to its fullest and best. Store cheese in a larder or cold room.

Yoghurt

Yoghurt is the cultured milk product that is most easily made at home (see page 25). There are long traditions of eating yoghurt in Turkish, Greek and Balkan countries where it is said to aid longevity, with wonderful pictures of gnarled men and women used by commercial producers to emphasize this point. Yoghurt is also traditionally made in India where it is used in a drink, lassi, and the delicious raita, a sauce that has much in common with the Greek tzatziki, both being made from yoghurt, cucumber and mint – surely a case of synergy of ingredients.

Milk becomes yoghurt due to the action of the bacterium *Lactobacillus bulgaricus*. This causes the milk to acidify and thicken. Greek yoghurt is then strained through muslin to give a fat content of 10%. Other yoghurts vary in fat content, with the very low-fat or non-fat yoghurts thickened using gum or other thickening agents. My thoughts are always that it is better to have one spoonful of delicious full-fat yoghurt than any amount of its pallid low-fat alternative.

Yoghurt is best kept in a cold room or fridge.

Butter

Anyone who has popped a carton of double cream into a mixer and left it running by mistake knows how to make butter! In a dairy, cream is skimmed from the milk and churned until it separates into butterfat and buttermilk. This is not the cultured product sold as buttermilk today, but just the liquid left when the butterfat globules combine to form a mass.

Butter is then often salted, though much less so now in these days of refrigeration, and kneaded to form pats. If this is done by hand, wooden butter paddles are used. Butter can be pressed into moulds, and in times past each dairy would have a distinctive decorative mould to show where it had been produced.

Soft, or 'ready-to-spread', butter is a mixture of butter and vegetable oil.

Butter can safely be stored in a cold larder.

Cream

Cream is the butterfat that sits on top of un-homogenized milk. In the UK cream is sold in any number of concentrations, the main two being single cream which is 18% fat, and double cream which is 48%. The uniquely British speciality cream, clotted cream, is a heat-treated cream that comes in at a magnificent 85% fat.

Cream is perishable and is best stored in the fridge.

Equipment

Very little special equipment is needed to make the cheeses and yoghurts I have given in these recipes. It is important, though, to remember that when using any dairy products everything must be spotlessly clean. Metal spoons are preferable to wooden ones, and glass or china bowls are best. The dishwasher will clean thoroughly, but hot soapy water works well too.

The muslin through which you drain your cheese must be spotlessly clean also. To scald muslin, place the cloth in a bowl, cover with boiling water and leave for 60 seconds. If you have no muslin for draining your cheese, it's safe to use a freshly washed and ironed tea towel (dish towel). The heat of the iron will kill off any bugs.

I save plastic cream and yoghurt pots for storing yoghurt in. I wash these well, often using the sterilizing tablets commonly sold to sterilize babies' bottles.

❧❧❧

Dairy products are rich and varied, they add wonderful flavours to our foods, and delight our palates with their diversity. And I only have to think of life without whipped-cream-filled meringues, molten cheese on toast, strawberry smoothies and Greek yoghurt drizzled with honey to acknowledge my commitment to them...

This butter is wonderfully versatile. Spread it on bread, let it melt over grilled meat and fish, or toss it into new potatoes or lightly cooked summer vegetables. It can be rolled in clingfilm (plastic wrap) and frozen, when it keeps well. Removing the pith and seeds of the chilli will lessen the heat.

Place all the ingredients in a food processor and whiz until everything is finely chopped and well blended. The butter can be served as is in a dish, or prepared as below.

Spread out on your work surface a double layer of clingfilm about 30cm/12in square. Scrape the butter on to the clingfilm then roll up to form a sausage. Tie off one end and then squeeze the butter up to give a roll about 15cm/6in long. Chill before cutting into slices. The butter also freezes well, double-wrapped in clingfilm and then stored in a plastic bag, or simply pressed into a lidded plastic freezer container of the right size.

Keep for two weeks in the fridge, or up to three months in the freezer.

Chilli- & Herb-spiked Garlic Butter

Makes approx 300g/10½oz

1 fresh red chilli
225g/8oz/2 sticks lightly salted butter
a handful of fresh coriander (cilantro), chervil, tarragon or parsley leaves
freshly ground black pepper
finely grated zest of 1 lime
2 plump garlic cloves, peeled

Other flavoured butters:
Almost any seasoning you enjoy can be incorporated into seasoned butters. Here are some of my other favourites:

❖ Orange, fennel and chive works well with pork
❖ Lemon, caper and black pepper for fish
❖ Smoked paprika, garlic and parsley for chicken
❖ Juniper, orange and mace for venison or other game steaks

Make as above and store, well-wrapped in clingfilm, in the freezer. Keep for 3 months.

Fresh Cheese with Garlic & Herbs

Makes approx. 500g/18oz

500ml/18fl oz/2¼ cups full-fat (whole)
    milk cottage cheese
500ml/18fl oz/2¼ cups full-fat (whole)
    milk yoghurt
500ml/18fl oz/2¼ cups double (heavy)
    cream
2 garlic cloves, peeled and crushed
2–3 tablespoons chopped fresh herbs
sea salt and freshly ground
    black pepper

Whilst it's not really feasible to make a hard cheese at home, this soft fresh cheese is simple to make and delicious to eat.

Don't use skimmed milk products to make it lower in fat, as this will give a thinner, flavourless finish. Choose whatever herbs you like. Sometimes I use just one variety, basil or tarragon say, and at other times a mixture of flat-leaf parsley, coriander (cilantro) and even some tender thyme leaves.

Combine the cottage cheese, yoghurt and cream in a food processor. Purée until completely smooth. Add the garlic and chopped herbs, and season to taste.

Line a colander or sieve with a double layer of scalded cheesecloth or muslin, and set this over a bowl. Scoop the mixture into the sieve, and cover loosely with a cloth. Set aside to drain at room temperature until the cheese becomes dry and firm (about 12 hours). It is ready when no more liquid drips from it.

Tip the cheese into a pot or place in a clean dish. Cover and refrigerate until ready to use.

The cheese will mature in flavour if left for 24 hours before serving, and is best then, but it can be kept in the fridge for up to a week.

Feta is a wonderfully versatile cheese, taking as it does to being served plain in a salad or as in this recipe, where it is marinated and left to absorb the flavours before use. Feta is traditionally used in Greek salads where it is mixed with cucumber and tomatoes, but it is also excellent crumbled into couscous, quinoa and rice salads, and sprinkled over baked squash or ratatouille.

The amount of oil needed will depend on the jar you use and how tightly you pack the cheese.

Cut the feta into 1cm/½in cubes and place in a suitably sized sterilized jar (see page 165). Mix the dry marinade ingredients together and add them to the cheese. Now pour in enough oil to cover. Screw on the lid and invert the jar gently a couple of times.

Place in a cold larder or a fridge for a week before using. This cheese keeps for up to a month.

Marinated Feta

Serves 4–6

200g/7oz feta cheese
finely grated zest of ½ lemon
2 garlic cloves, peeled and crushed
1 dried red chilli, crushed
coarsely ground black pepper
1 tablespoon dried mint, crumbled
100–200ml/3½–7fl oz/¼–½ cup extra
   virgin olive oil

Potted Blue Cheese

Makes 450g/1lb

225g/8oz/1¾ cups blue cheese, crumbled
115g/4oz/1 cup Cheddar cheese, finely
   grated
115g/4oz/1 cup curd cheese
1 teaspoon mild mustard

Potting cheese makes good use of any unsightly odds and ends that you might have left in the larder. I use the remains of the Stilton after Christmas, but any blue cheese will work well. Potted cheese is good as an appetizer served with crackers, or used as a stuffing for grilled or baked pears served with a leaf salad. Try also spooning the cheese into jacket potatoes or on top of a steak, hot off the grill.

As you are, by definition, using a mouldy cheese, be aware that this potted cheese keeps for only about one week.

Place all the ingredients in the goblet of a blender or food processor and mix until smooth. If you like a rougher texture, pound it in a mortar.

Either divide the mixture between four to six small ramekins, or press into one larger ramekin. Cover, and leave for about 24 hours before eating to allow the flavours to develop.

Wanting to make this one day, but with no blue cheese, I increased the amount of cheddar and added a teaspoon of crushed celery seeds – it was delicious.

This is a very easy cheese to make at home, and each time I try it, I vary the flavours. I first ate paneer at a vegetarian restaurant serving a mixture of foods from the north of India. The paneer takes the place of meat in a vegetarian diet, but I have also eaten it mixed with fish and shellfish in a spicy sauce, and it not only adds flavour and texture, it extends a more costly protein. Although delicious used in stir-fries and curries, paneer can also be crumbled on to pizzas and used in sandwiches.

The main points when making paneer are that you use whole milk and that you drain the curd thoroughly. The milk is heated, then a souring agent is added to form curds. I have given several options below. If using yoghurt or buttermilk, it may be necessary to heat the milk a little longer once they have been added, whereas the lemon juice works at once. A light vinegar, such as rice wine vinegar, can be used in place of lemon juice. Fresh herbs can be used, but I find I get a better result with dried.

Draining the paneer at first over a sieve then under a heavy weight is a very important stage, so do take time to do this. Only when all the whey has been pressed out will the cheese be firm enough to slice.

Spicy *Paneer* Cheese

Makes approx. 400g/14oz

1.5 litres/2¾ pints/6 cups full-fat (whole) milk
2–3 tablespoons Greek-style yoghurt, or 100ml/3½fl oz/½ cup buttermilk or 2–3 tablespoons lemon juice

Seasonings (choose some or all of those below)
about 1 garlic clove, peeled and crushed
2.5cm/1in fresh ginger root, peeled and grated
½ teaspoon ground cumin
½ teaspoon fine sea salt
½ teaspoon freshly ground black pepper
dried thyme, oregano or mint

Have ready a sieve or colander lined with a double layer of scalded muslin or cheesecloth. Place it over a bowl.

Heat the milk in a large saucepan. Once the milk is boiling add the yoghurt, buttermilk or lemon juice and stir. Add your seasonings. As soon as the mixture separates, forming curds and whey, remove the pan from the heat and pour the mixture into the prepared sieve. Allow as much whey to drain away as possible then gather up the corners of the muslin and make them into a sort of parcel. Place this on a rack over a bowl or dish and then place a board on top, finished with a heavy weight. Place in a cool larder or fridge and leave for at least 1 hour.

Once the cheese is dry, cut into cubes and store these in a jar or bowl of lightly salted water in a cold larder or the fridge for up to four days.

Home-made Yoghurt

Makes approx. 800ml/1½ pints

650ml/22fl oz/2¾ cups full-fat (whole)
    organic milk
4 tablespoons organic skimmed
    milk powder
either 1 small 150g/5oz pot or 2 heaped
    tablespoons natural yoghurt

So simple and so delicious you'll wonder why you didn't try this before. Home-made yoghurt has a pure flavour and an acidity that makes for an especially pleasing dish.

I do think that organic is the way to go here. I use full-fat (whole) milk with the addition of dried skimmed milk, the organic version of which is now readily available. I make my first batch using a small pot of bought natural, organic yoghurt, and then reserve a couple of spoonfuls of my own yoghurt to make the next batch. The culture lasts for about five to six batches. When you feel your yoghurt culture is tiring, just make the next batch with a new pot of yoghurt.

I use a wide-necked vacuum flask to make my yoghurt. Any flask will do, but a wide-necked one allows you to spoon the yoghurt out. I also find that the 750ml/ 26fl oz flasks keep the culture warm for as long as it needs to make the yoghurt. Smaller flasks tend to cool too quickly, giving a thinner, less crisp-flavoured yoghurt. I am unable to find a litre/ 1¾ pint flask, which would be ideal.

As ever, utensils must be spotlessly clean.

Fill your flask with boiling water, then put to one side.

Mix the milk and milk powder in a small pan over a low heat. Heat until warm. You can use a thermometer but I just test a little on a spoon. It should feel a little hotter than tepid.

Now stir in the yoghurt, mixing well.

Empty the flask of water, pour in the yoghurt mix and put on the lid. Leave the flask overnight, I find 24 hours suits me.

Open the flask, spoon the yoghurt into a clean container, and chill.

Home-made yoghurt is wonderful in a number of dishes. I sometimes strain it to give a thicker consistency. Line a sieve with scalded cheesecloth or muslin and place over a bowl. Pour in the yoghurt and allow the mixture to drip. You can strain for a short time to give a thicker but still stirrable yoghurt or leave to drip overnight to make a fresh, cheese-like dish.

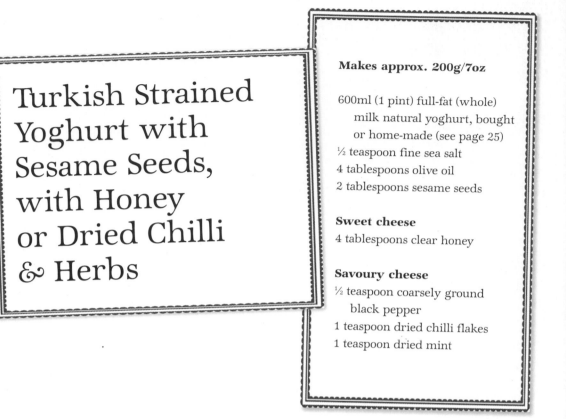

Turkish Strained Yoghurt with Sesame Seeds, with Honey or Dried Chilli & Herbs

Makes approx. 200g/7oz

600ml (1 pint) full-fat (whole)
    milk natural yoghurt, bought
    or home-made (see page 25)
½ teaspoon fine sea salt
4 tablespoons olive oil
2 tablespoons sesame seeds

Sweet cheese
4 tablespoons clear honey

Savoury cheese
½ teaspoon coarsely ground
    black pepper
1 teaspoon dried chilli flakes
1 teaspoon dried mint

Once you have made your own home-made yoghurt, you can take the dish a stage further by straining it to give a softish cheese, known in the Middle East as labneh. *This can be flavoured in a number of ways.*

Line a colander or sieve with scalded muslin or cheesecloth, and set over a bowl.

Beat the yoghurt and salt together and spoon the mixture into the mould. Cover with a cloth and allow to drain for 24 hours.

Meanwhile heat the oil and, when hot, add the sesame seeds. Cook until pale gold (they will continue to cook as they cool),

and quickly remove from the heat. Leave in the oil.

If making the sweet cheese, simply allow the seeded oil to cool. If making a savoury cheese, add the black pepper, chilli flakes and mint to the seeded oil, stir and allow the oil to cool.

To serve the *labneh*, remove it from the sieve or colander, take off the cheesecloth, and place it on a dish. Pour over the seeded oil and, for the sweet version, spoon on the honey.

Serve the savoury cheese with flat bread, and the sweet one spooned into dessert dishes accompanied by sponge fingers or shortbread.

CHARCUTERIE

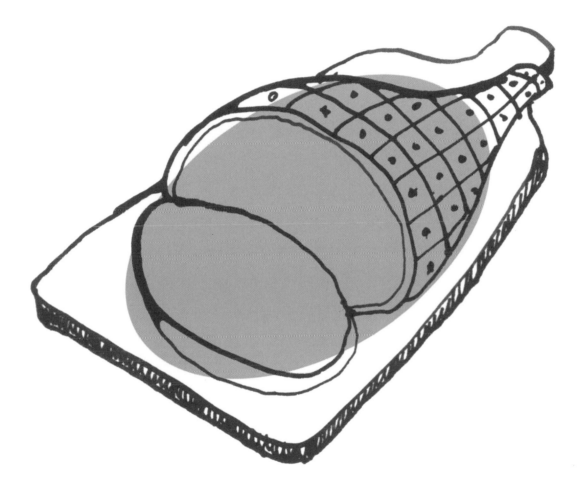

Introduction

The word '*charcuterie*' may be French, but the art of creating delicious and wonderful foods from all parts of the animal is very much an international one.

It is here that the noble pig rises head and shoulder above other beasts, for whilst the standing rib roast is said to be Britain's crowning glory, beef must take second place to pork when it comes to making pâtés, pies, brawns and sausages.

What makes the pig king is the quality and quantity of its fat. Pork fat is sublime, with a rich texture and mild creamy taste. Indeed, throughout Europe you will find examples of foods where the fat takes precedence over the lean meat. The Spanish *jamón ibérico* is probably the most expensive ham in today's market. The special *ibérico* pig is carefully raised, growing slowly and spending its final months in oak forests in central Spain, where it grazes on fallen acorns, earning the appellation '*bellota*' (acorn). This feeding regime is said to give the pork its wonderful flavour, but when carving these rather scrawny hams it is the fat that is most looked for and most carefully sliced. The delicate sweetness of this melting gently on your tongue is one of my most wonderful food moments.

Lardo, a cured, air-dried Italian delicacy, is simply a slab of fat, again thinly sliced and served with bread. Butchers are judged on the excellence of their *lardo* and guard their recipes zealously.

In France there is a wonderful culture of *charcuteries* – shops who make all manner of dishes to eat at home. Long before the Indian takeaway became the Friday night option, slices of *jambon persillé*, spoonfuls of rillettes and morsels of foie gras were bought with pride to serve at one's own table.

In Britain, we have a history of excellent pork butchers making sausages and regional specialities such as brawn, haslet, faggots and Bath chaps. These recipes, too, are guarded by their creators. Indeed, the butcher from whom my mother bought sausages when I was at school quarrelled with his sons and so refused to give them his magic recipe. As a result, when he died, the secret of his wonderful crumbly herb-infused sausages died with him!

Meat for Charcuterie

Many cuts are suitable for *charcuterie*, and the best way to work out which cut to use it to ask yourself if the cut could be served simply roasted. If so, that would have been its fate. *Charcuterie* developed as a way of making use of the less prime cuts, everything but the squeak!

Pork

Pork is the most versatile meat when it comes to making pies, pâtés and sausages. It is the basic ingredient on which so many classic recipes are built. For even if you want to make game pie or venison sausages, the addition of fatty pork, most often from the belly, improves both the flavour and texture.

Always buy outdoor-reared, free-range pork. Not only will the flavour be incomparable, but you will know that you are supporting farmers who have considerably higher standards of animal husbandry and welfare than those who produce pork for the mass market. I am a committed carnivore, but like to think that the meat I eat has been carefully and intelligently looked after. Rare-breed pork sits at the top of the tree, and whilst it is more costly you are paying for quality and, of course, when making *charcuterie*, you are using the less sought-after cuts.

It is pork belly that one uses most often in making sausages, terrines and pies. Pork back fat is an excellent alternative if only the fat is called for, but in these days of lean pigs it is not readily available.

Every bit of the pig can be used from the snout to the tail; I recently ate deep-fried pigs' ears with a type of tartare sauce, and they were very good indeed. Trotters split and simmered with seasoning vegetables make a rich gelatinous stock that can be used to fill the air gaps in pork pies and cover cooked meats like potted hough.

Pig's liver is the base of most coarse country-style pâtés for, whilst it has a strong flavour, it has an essential richness that adds a luscious quality to the finished dish.

Ducks, Geese and Chicken

As ducks and geese have a lot of naturally occurring fat, these birds are best for preserving in confit or as rillettes and pâtés. Duck and goose fat is highly valued and can be collected and saved for roasting vegetables and enriching casseroles.

Chicken breasts can be used to make *boudin blanc* (see page 42), and the fattier thigh meat makes wonderful potted chicken, perfect for a summer picnic with crispbread and pickles. But it is chicken livers that are most useful. I am always amazed at how little this luxurious-tasting liver costs, and how versatile chicken livers are.

Duck and goose livers make excellent pâtés, too, but are more difficult to find in quantity. Nevertheless, when I buy a duck or goose, I make a simple pâté by simmering shallots in plenty of butter, adding the trimmed duck or goose liver, cooking until still faintly pink in the centre then flaming with brandy. All that is left to do is to season well with salt and pepper and whiz the mixture in a blender or processor. Potted in a ramekin, you may not have enough to feed the family but for you, with a glass of wine, some crisp toast and a good book... Heaven.

All livers should be well trimmed and any green staining from ruptured bile ducts cut away and discarded.

Veal

Traditionally used in veal and ham pies, veal is a meat I believe we should be eating more of. The days of veal crates are long past in the UK, and pink or rose veal is widely available. It seems to me a tragedy that male dairy calves, a by-product of the dairy industry, are discarded as waste rather than enjoyed as meat, all because we have an outdated notion that eating veal is cruel. My mantra is that anyone who drinks milk must eat veal. No farmer wants to celebrate the safe delivery of a calf by shooting it moments later for its simple failing of being the wrong gender.

Lamb, Mutton and Beef

Only a few cuts of these butchers' meats are generally used in *charcuterie*. Beef tongues are salted then cooked and pressed (see page 46). They have a soft texture and delicate flavour, and are an essential part of any cold meat selection.

Lambs' tongues are most usually cooked and served hot, but can be prepared in the same fashion as beef tongue. Minced lamb and mutton make good tasty sausages. *Merguez* and *sheftalia* (see pages 41 and 43) both use the fatty lamb from the breast or shoulder. Lamb's liver has a mild flavour and is excellent for pâtés.

Game

Both feathered and furred game – rabbit, venison, pheasant, partridge and mallard to name a few – are excellent for pâtés, pies and potted meats. As game is usually low in intrinsic fat, it is necessary to add extra to achieve the best taste and texture. Pork fat is most commonly used.

To give a contrast of texture, and to make the most of the prime parts of the meat, I like to cut the breasts from birds or fillets from rabbit and venison, and reserve them. I then take the rest of the meat from the carcasses and mince it to make a farce. When it comes to making a terrine or pie, I fill the dish or crust with half the farce and then lay in the fillets, topping with the remaining farce.

When cooked and sliced you have lovely pale strips of deliciously moist meat in the centre of the dish.

If I am given several mallards or other wild ducks, I often cut the breasts off to pan-fry, then make confit of the legs using the recipe on page 154.

Equipment

Very little special equipment is needed to start making your own pâtés, pies and sausages, but the following are some pieces of kit that will prove useful.

Mincer

Either electric or hand-cranked, a mincer will give your pâtés and pies an excellent, even texture. While your butcher can mince the meats for you, you may find him reluctant to mince game and chicken. These can be chopped in a food processor, but a mincer is the tool of choice. If you have a free-standing electric mixer, you may be able to buy a mincing attachment.

Remember that minced meat spoils more rapidly then uncut meat as it has a greater surface area.

Sausage Fillers

Mechanical sausage fillers are available for the enthusiast. I might suggest you will need to make a lot of sausages to warrant the expense, but there is no doubt that once you get the knack of filling the sausages, these machines do give a professional finish.

To link the sausage you need to take a length of the filled casing and twist it to form a loop. You then pull the long line of casing through the loop, twist this and continue as above. You will soon get the hang of it and will create long rows of double sausages. Chipolatas are linked in threes and, while I have spent many hours trying, I am fairly useless at this.

If you really want to embrace sausage-making and you buy your meat from your local butcher, he may well give you a lesson. It's worth asking.

Cast-iron Terrines

Cooking a terrine in a lidded cast-iron dish just seems to give it an extra something, but a loaf tin from your baking drawer will work just as well. Usually pâtés and terrines are cooked in a bain-marie – this is simply a large roasting dish half filled with water – or enough water to come halfway up the terrine when it is put in the dish.

Storing Cooked Charcuterie

If you have a cold room or larder this will be perfectly adequate to store most cooked meat. Sausages should always be stored in the fridge, as should the chicken liver parfait on page 49.

The usual rules apply about never mixing cooked meat with raw, and you will have to bear in mind what has happened to the meat. If, for instance, you have taken a spoonful of pâté from the dish, you will have broken the seal and opened the pâté to the air so it becomes more vulnerable to bacteria.

I have a horror of use-by and best-before dates. They threaten, but with only half the information. 'Use by...', or what happens? 'Best before', but are they totally rubbish after or just not so nice? Will you have a slightly less tasty meal or be rather ill? This is what we need to know, not an arbitrary date that no-one really understands.

So it is important to have a little knowledge about what makes food spoil. Temperature alone is not sufficient, but a warm room will allow the food to heat and so give a better breeding ground for bacteria. If you lick the spoon before taking a second helping, you add a whole host of pathogens to the dish. The importance of serving spoons which are used for that purpose alone should be stressed. Making sure all the pots, dishes, spoons and cloths you use are spotlessly clean is essential. It's all just common sense without the ghastliness of health and safety.

Few things speak more eloquently of plenty than a glazed ham. Proudly sitting atop their stands, cooked whole, bone-in hams have made a reappearance at delicatessen and supermarket counters recently. Hand-carved, they are a real link to our past, when every pantry would hold a selection of such delicacies as game pie, pressed tongue and ham.

Cooking ham is quite simple: simmer it, covered with water, in your largest pot until tender. That will take about 20 minutes per 500g/18oz. Lift it from the water, allow to cool, then skin it. For an unglazed ham, you dress the fat with golden breadcrumbs.

For a glazed ham you can become even more fancy. I like a mixture of mustard and marmalade: the mustard starch combines with the marmalade to form a crust which has a glossy finish. Honey works well, too, and you can stud the ham with cloves should you so desire. I hate cloves with a passion so I leave this bit out.

Once the ham has cooled, remove the skin, leaving as much fat on the ham as possible. This layer of fat protects the meat and, whilst you might not wish to eat it, remember that it is the fat that is most prized by aficionados of *jamón ibérico*.

Using a sharp knife, score through the fat making a diamond pattern all over the ham. If you're using cloves, now is the time to stick one clove into each diamond shape.

Preheat the oven to 170°C/340°F/Gas Mark 3. Mix your chosen glaze ingredients together to form a stiffish paste.

Place the ham in a roasting dish and spoon over the glaze. Bake in the preheated oven for 10 minutes per 500g/18oz, basting as often as you can.

Cool, transfer to a clean dish and store in a cold pantry for up to two weeks.

Sticky Glazed Ham

Serves up to 20, depending on weight

1 cooked ham (you can cook your own or buy a cooked, undressed ham from the butcher)
cloves (optional)

Glaze 1
300g/10½oz/1¾ cups marmalade
3–4 tablespoons dry mustard powder

Glaze 2
175g/6oz/¾ cup soft brown sugar
2 tablespoons sherry or orange juice
2 tablespoons plain (all-purpose) flour

Glaze 3
400g/14oz/1¾ cups redcurrant jelly
finely grated zest of 1 orange and 1 lemon
2 tablespoons port

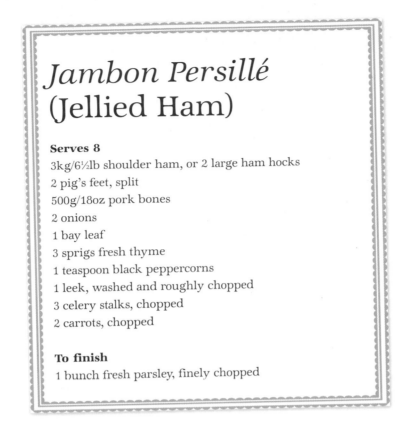

Jambon Persillé (Jellied Ham)

Serves 8

3kg/6½lb shoulder ham, or 2 large ham hocks

2 pig's feet, split

500g/18oz pork bones

2 onions

1 bay leaf

3 sprigs fresh thyme

1 teaspoon black peppercorns

1 leek, washed and roughly chopped

3 celery stalks, chopped

2 carrots, chopped

To finish

1 bunch fresh parsley, finely chopped

French charcuteries *always have large bowls of this ham on show. But in the Midlands of England, they also cook a wide range of cured pork dishes, and parslied ham is one of the traditional ones. My recipe owes more to the French, though, as I like a highish proportion of jelly.*

If the ham is very salty, soak it for 24 hours, changing the water once or twice. To avoid getting too much scum on the stock, immerse the pig's feet and bones in boiling water to blanch them for 5 minutes, then drain and rinse well.

Put the ham, prepared bones and pig's feet, onions, bay, thyme, peppercorns, leek, celery and carrots into a large casserole dish or your biggest saucepan, and cover with cold water. Bring to the boil and simmer for 2½–3½ hours, or until the ham is very tender. Try to keep the stock as scum-free as possible by skimming with a slotted spoon

dipped in hot water. If the level of the stock drops, top up with boiling water. The solids should be covered at all times.

Once the meat is cooked, lift the ham from the stock. Allow to cool a little then remove all the meat, discarding the skin and bones.

Strain 1 litre/1¾ pints/3½ cups of the stock into a clean pan. (Freeze the rest for soups, etc.) Bring the stock to the boil and simmer until it reduces by about one-third.

Meanwhile, dice the meat and arrange in a spotlessly clean glass or china bowl.

Stir the parsley into the reduced stock, and pour over the ham. Chill until set, then store in the fridge until needed. This will keep for up to seven days in the fridge.

Serve the ham either as part of a 'cold meats' plate with salad, piccalilli and crusty bread, or spooned over dressed leaves as a starter or light lunch. Some sherry vinegar works well in the dressing.

Sausages

The best sausages to buy are those made by your local butcher. All good butchers take a great pride in their sausages, and make them in small batches. This is how they do it.

The fairly fatty pork shoulder meat is minced (ground), along with a proportion of belly (usually 9kg/20lb to 1kg/2¼lb), then seasoned and kneaded by hand to extend the protein. This is the bit that changes simple minced pork into sausage meat and gives the finished sausage its slightly bouncy texture. Rusk, water and seasoning additions vary according to the type of sausage being made; adding a small dose of preservatives to sausages extends the shelf life beyond a day. The meat is then packed by machine into casings and the sausages are hand-linked.

Rusk is used in butcher's sausages as it does not contain yeast; at home I use home-made breadcrumbs. The meat, at best free-range pork, is always hand-trimmed, which means removing all gristle, sinew, those dreaded tubes and any glands which, if left in, could taint the taste of the meat. When I make simple pork and herb sausages for my toad in the hole, I don't bother with casings. I simply shape the sausages by hand and lightly pan-fry them. I think this lack of casing actually improves the texture of the dish.

I also like to make *merguez*, a French/North African lamb sausage. You need quite fatty mature lamb for these sausages, so winter is the best time to make them. Seasoned with paprika, chilli, herbs and salt, these sausages are delicious eaten with couscous and a vegetable stew. Again, casings aren't strictly necessary but should you have a sausage filler and long to try to make your own links, buy the casings from your butcher.

You must start with spotlessly clean utensils. Sausages, like any other much-handled minced meat product, can easily be contaminated, but if you follow good kitchen hygiene practice, you should have no problems.

Meats

As I have said above, never put rubbish in a sausage. Choose good-quality meat, free-range if possible, and remember that fat is an essential part of the mix. The shoulder meat of both pork and lamb is best for sausages, and if making beef or game sausages, you might need to add pork back fat at a ratio of 100g/3½oz fat to every 500g/18oz lean meat. If you want to make chicken sausages (not the *boudins* on page 42), use thigh meat and add a little minced unsmoked bacon.

Seasonings

You can experiment with different seasonings, adding chilli, herbs, finely diced apple or some finely chopped leek that has been softened in olive oil. More robust flavours can make a delightful change, so try pork and fresh ginger, or lamb with juniper. Saffron works with chicken, and ground spices such as cumin and coriander work well with game.

Casings

Sausage casings are available quite readily in both synthetic and natural forms. Natural casings give, I think, a better bite to your sausage. The casings are the small intestines of ox, sheep and pigs. The lamb casings are the smallest, and are generally used for chipolata sausages. They tend to be more delicate than hog or ox casings, which give larger 'banger'-type sausages. The filling for the casings can be the same, although, interestingly, the sausages will taste a little different when cooked.

When using casings, they should be soaked according to your supplier's instructions, then thoroughly washed, with running cold water flushed through the entire length. (Synthetic casings, mostly made from bovine protein, need much less preparation, and also can be stored for longer.)

It is best to use an electric sausage filler if you decide to use casings. I find that greasing the filler tube with a little vegetable oil helps you to slip the casings on more easily. The manufacturer will give instructions as to how to load the filler and fill the casings, but take care to get the casings on tightly and pack the fillers as evenly as possible.

Filling sausage casings by hand, either with a hand-cranked sausage filler or a funnel, is difficult as the sausage skins need to be evenly packed. I don't think the result is worth the effort so if you decide not to use skins, and mostly that is what I decide, simply form sausage shapes with slightly damp hands.

Caul

Caul, a fatty membrane which covers the internal organs of animals such as cows, sheep and pigs, is an excellent substitute for casings when making sausages at home. It is used to wrap and add succulence to rissoles and other meat dishes. Soak well in cold water before use, taking each sheet and carefully opening it up fully. The technique is very similar to using clingfilm (plastic wrap). Both pig's and lamb's caul is available to order from your butcher.

Linking sausages

Linking sausages looks wonderfully simple but takes a dexterous hand. Essentially you need to decide how large you would like your sausages to be, about 13cm/5in is good, and then pinch the filled casing at this mark. Twist it to form the end of that sausage and the start of the next. Make your next sausage in the same fashion but twist it in the opposite direction. Butchers now form links by creating a loop and threading the last sausage back through the length to make the next part of the chain.

❖ Note

Sausages are a fresh product. Home-made sausages must be stored in the fridge, and should be eaten within 48 hours of making. They must be cooked through. Butcher's sausages contain preservatives that extend their shelf life.

Pork & Herb Sausages

**Makes 1kg/2¼lb sausages
(16 large, 24 small)**

800g/1¾lb pork shoulder meat
250g/9oz belly of pork, rind and bones
    removed
1 teaspoon fine sea salt
½ teaspoon freshly ground black pepper
1 teaspoon freeze-dried mixed herbs
85g/3oz/1½ cups brown breadcrumbs
sausage casing of choice

An excellent everyday sausage, and perhaps the best sausage for first-time sausage makers. They are good with mash and onion gravy, work well in toad in the hole, and are delicious shaped as patties and cooked for breakfast.

Cut the meat into pieces and put through the finest blade of the mincer once.

In a large bowl mix the remaining ingredients into the meat, kneading it for about 4–5 minutes by hand. The mixture will become sticky and start to cling together.

Thread large sausage casing on to the large tube of the sausage filler, and fill the casing with mixture. Form into links of 13cm/5in sausages. Store the sausages in a clean dish for 24 hours before cooking, then use within 24 hours.

These sausages can be grilled under a moderate heat, turning often until golden brown, or fried over a low heat. I also bake them in a moderate oven at 180ºC/350ºF/ Gas Mark 4 for approximately 20 minutes.

If you are not using cases, these sausages can be cooked and eaten on the day they are made. Do try other seasonings, grated fresh ginger is particularly tasty.

Merguez Sausages

Makes 450g/1lb sausages (about 6–8)

450g/1lb fatty lamb, skinned (boned breast of
    lamb is ideal)
1 tablespoon hot paprika
1 tablespoon sweet paprika
½ tablespoon each of garlic salt, ground cumin,
    ground coriander and freshly ground
    black pepper
2 tablespoons lukewarm water

*These tasty sausages hail from North
Africa and are made with mutton or lamb.
They are excellent grilled over hot coals and
served with couscous and chopped mint.*

Cut the meat into small pieces and pass it
twice through a mincer.

Place the meat with the spices in a large
bowl and knead everything together with
your hands for 2–3 minutes. The meat
becomes a little sticky, though not as sticky
as when making pork sausages.

Slip narrow sausage casing on to a fine
tube sausage filler and fill the casing.
(The *merguez* mixture can also be shaped
by hand into long sausage shapes and
wrapped in caul fat.)

Twist the sausages into links of 20cm/8in
sausages and place in the fridge. Cook the
same day or wrap and freeze.

Merguez in skins are best cooked under
a moderate grill. Unskinned sausages can
be fried without additional fat. Cook for
10–15 minutes depending on thickness.

Veal & Chicken *Boudins Blanc* with Green Peppercorns

Makes 6–8 sausages

225g/8oz boneless skinless chicken breast
    meat
225g/8oz minced (ground) veal
2 tablespoons double (heavy) cream
2 egg whites
¼ teaspoon fine sea salt
1 teaspoon green peppercorns

To serve
a little unsalted butter

Boudin blanc is a French white sausage made from chicken or veal. Here, the finely minced (ground) meat is mixed with egg white and a little cream and poached. I like to gently pan-fry these elegant boudins, and serve them with a little well-seasoned mashed potato (diluted with warm milk until it is almost a purée), and a tarragon beurre blanc.

If you have trouble finding British pink veal, use 450g/1lb chicken breast. This recipe works best if all the ingredients are well chilled.

Mince, process or finely chop the chicken breast. Place in a food processor, then add the veal and process again to ensure the two meats are well mixed. Add the cream, egg whites and salt. Process for a further 1–2 minutes then turn the mixture into a bowl and chill for 1 hour.

Mix the well-drained peppercorns into the *boudin* mix.

Cut 6 to 8 pieces of clingfilm (plastic wrap), each roughly 13cm/5in square. Place about 2 tablespoons of the *boudin* mixture on to a square of film then roll it into a sausage shape, using the film. Once the shape is as you like it, completely enclose the sausage with clingfilm and tie a knot in each end. This can be done either by knotting the film or using a piece of cotton.

Bring a large pan of water to the boil and place the *boudins* in this. Simmer for 12 minutes then remove from the water, drain and allow to cool. Once cold, chill.

When you want to serve, remove the film from the *boudins*. Heat a little butter in a heavy-bottomed frying pan and fry the sausages gently until they are heated through and lightly coloured on all sides.

Sheftalia

**Serves 6 as a main course,
more as part of a barbecue meal**

1kg/2¼lb minced (ground) lamb or pork
175g/6oz/1 cup very finely chopped onion
55g/2oz/scant 1½ cups chopped fresh
    flat-leaf parsley
1 teaspoon each of ground cinnamon,
    ground cumin and freshly ground
    black pepper
1 teaspoon fine sea salt
lamb's caul

*This Greek sausage is always made at
home and has a coarser texture than
a British sausage. Excellent grilled on
a barbecue, you must make sure the
sheftalias are cooked through.*

Mix the meat, onion, parsley and spices
together. Knead the mixture lightly until
it begins to bind together.

Take a small handful of the mixture
and shape into a sausage approximately
10cm/4in in length and a little fatter than
your thumb.

Wrap this in a piece of caul, making sure
the whole surface is covered, and cutting
away any excess caul. Place on a baking
sheet. Continue until all the mixture is
used. Chill until needed.

Heat a grill or barbecue until hot then
cook the *sheftalias* slowly until well
browned and cooked through. This will
take about 15–20 minutes.

Serve with a good squeeze of lemon
juice, salad and warmed pitta bread.

Game Terrine

Serves 6–8 as a hefty starter

85g/3oz/¾ stick butter
2 large shallots, peeled and chopped
1 plump garlic clove, peeled and crushed
600g/1lb 5oz game meat
450g/1lb rindless fat belly of pork
250g/9oz chicken livers, trimmed
1 teaspoon fresh thyme leaves
1 teaspoon chopped fresh sage leaves
2 tablespoons brandy
sea salt and freshly ground black pepper

To finish
approx. 225g/8oz thinly cut streaky bacon
2 bay leaves

If you have a glut of feathered game and can't face plucking them, skinning is a great option. Once skinned, the birds are suitable for casseroles or for terrines.

The meat cut from three medium game birds weighs approximately 600g/1lb 5oz, but you can make up the quantities using extra pork or a few more chicken livers if necessary.

Melt the butter then gently fry the shallot and garlic until soft, about 5–7 minutes. Allow to cool.

Preheat oven to 160°C/320°F/Gas Mark 3.

Mince the game meat, pork and livers together twice, using the finest blade of the mincer. Place the meat in a large bowl and add the herbs, the butter, shallot and garlic mixture, brandy, salt and pepper. Beat the mixture well with a spoon then fry a small piece to taste. Correct seasoning, if necessary.

Remove the rind from the bacon slices and then stretch them slightly. To do this, lay the bacon on a board and, using the back of a heavy knife, run the blade along the bacon, pressing it out. Use to line a 1kg/2¼lb loaf tin – I have a cast-iron enamelled one with a lid. (If using thinly cut pancetta, this does not need to be stretched.) Press in the minced game mixture then cover the top with bacon. Lay the bay leaves on this, then cover closely with a double thickness of foil and the lid.

Place the terrine dish in a roasting tray half filled with cold water (a bain-marie), and cook in the preheated oven for 1¾ hours. The terrine will shrink from the sides of the tin. Cool, then refrigerate.

This terrine is best served after two days but will keep for up to a week in the fridge. Serve with crusty bread and tiny pickled gherkins.

Pressed Tongue

Serves 6–8

1 salted ox tongue, about 2.5–3kg/5½–6½lb
6 black peppercorns
2 bay leaves
1 onion, peeled and stuck with
   a few cloves
2 carrots, scrubbed and roughly sliced
2 celery stalks, roughly chopped

*Some things just taste better when
done at home, and this is one of them.
A traditional Christmas addition to
the groaning table, pressed tongue is a
wonderfully soft and flavourful meat to
serve on Boxing Day. It is excellent with
pickled walnuts and peppery watercress
or Cumberland sauce. It's also excellent
in sandwiches.*

Soak the tongue overnight in plenty of
cold water.

Drain and place the tongue in a deep
pan. Cover with cold water, bring to the
boil and drain.

Cover again with fresh cold water
and return to the boil. Add all the
remaining flavouring ingredients, and
simmer for about 3 hours, making sure
the meat is always covered by the liquid.
You may half cover the pan if you wish.

When the tongue is cooked, the small
bones come away easily and a skewer
inserted in the deepest part of the meat
slips in without resistance. Leave the
tongue to cool a little in the liquid.

It is easier to skin the tongue while still
a bit warm, so once it has cooled until it
is comfortable to handle, lift it from the
cooking liquid and place on a board. Using
a small sharp knife skin the tongue and
trim away some of the root, removing
the bones.

Place the tongue in a tongue press, if
using, following the directions (these are
available from specialist kitchen shops
and some supermarkets). If you don't have
a press, shape the tongue to fit in a deep
20cm/8in cake tin. Cover with a couple
of spoons of liquor and some greaseproof
(waxed) paper and then a small plate that
fits inside the tin, weighting it down with
a couple of heavy tins.

Continue cooling until cold enough to
put in the fridge, then chill for 24 hours
before taking from the mould and serving,
thinly sliced.

A rough country pâté with a fine flavour, this fits the bill for any supper party or picnic, or is good just to have to hand. I've used pink veal, believing strongly that we must use this delicious, kindly bred British veal as often as possible (see page 32), but you could use pork.

Mince the pork, veal, liver and half of the fat bacon together, using a mincer. Using a pestle and mortar, crush the garlic, peppercorns, juniper berries, mace and salt together.

Add these seasonings, as well as the wine and brandy, to the meat. Mix together thoroughly and leave in the fridge for the flavours to penetrate, if possible for up to 2 hours.

Preheat the oven to 150ºC/300ºF/Gas Mark 2.

Turn the mixture into a 1.2 litre/2 pint terrine and smooth the top. Cut the remaining fat bacon into strips and arrange it on top of the pâté.

Place the terrine in a roasting tray half full of cold water (a bain-marie), and cook uncovered in the preheated slow oven for about 1½–1¾ hours.

The pâté is cooked when it comes away from the side of the dish. There will be a pool of juice surrounding the pâté when it comes from the oven, which will set to a delicious jelly.

Store in the fridge for up to ten days.

Terrine de Campagne

Serves 6–8

450g/1lb fat belly of pork
450g/1lb lean British pink veal
225g/8oz pig's liver, trimmed
115g/4oz fat bacon rashers, rinded
2–3 plump garlic cloves, peeled
6 black peppercorns
6 juniper berries
¼ teaspoon ground mace
3 teaspoons sea salt, or to taste
75ml/2½fl oz/⅓ cup white wine
2 tablespoons brandy

Chicken Liver Parfait

Serves 6

500g/18oz chicken or duck livers, trimmed
4 egg yolks
1 teaspoon coarse sea salt
1 tablespoon each of port and brandy
freshly ground black pepper
1 garlic clove, peeled and crushed
1 tablespoon chopped fresh tarragon or chervil
225g/8oz/2 sticks butter, melted
approx. 115g/4oz clarified butter (see page 147)

Chicken livers are one of the world's most undervalued ingredients, bringing a real taste of luxury at a modest cost. This parfait is unashamedly rich and unctuous. Don't cut back on the butter and eggs, just eat a smaller portion if you can!

Do be aware that the uncooked mixture looks a little gruesome. Don't worry, though, once it's cooked it is delicious.

Preheat the oven to 150°C/300°F/Gas Mark 2, and use some extra butter to grease a 450g/1lb terrine dish or a 1 litre/1¾ pint soufflé dish or similar.

Put all the ingredients, except the two butters, into the bowl of a food processor and whiz them together until everything is finely chopped and well blended. You are looking to make this into as much of a liquid as possible.

Slowly pour in the melted butter and blend until mixed. Strain through a sieve into the buttered terrine dish. Place this in a bain-marie, a roasting pan filled with about 2.5cm/1in cold water.

Place this in the preheated oven and cook for about an hour or until the pâté, when felt in the middle, is slightly firm, and a paleish brown in colour.

Leave the pâté to cool in the terrine; pour over the clarified butter to seal completely. Store in the fridge for up to two weeks.

BREAD
AND PASTRY

Introduction

My love affair with bread-making goes a long way back. I have to admit that it started with a packet mix! When my children were young, and barbecues caused them great delight, I made up a packet of white bread mix, and gave it to them to pat into undeniably grubby flat breads, which we proceeded to cook on the grill.

Even that most ordinary of breads was delicious, eaten hot and stuffed with barbecued meats. Thereafter, bread-making became something I regularly did with the children, both mine and those that came to play. I found it a wonderful way of keeping small children happy for hours, and somehow made less mess than vibrantly coloured salt dough. It also had the added benefit that the end results could be taken home and eaten.

This early bread-making soon moved on to rather more everyday baking when I would experiment with different loaves and types of yeast. I wish I could say that all my experiments were a success, but I would be fibbing. There are still pigeons in North London with beaks bent from the day I threw them my early, discarded hot cross buns... I persevered, though, and soon had a sourdough mother quietly fermenting in the fridge.

The real joy to me of baking is that you only need to know and follow a few basic principles, and the recipe will never let you down. I have often served a deli-bought meal but added my own bread, and it is the bread that my guest remembered. There is another virtue to this craft and that is that making bread at home is very cost-effective. You can make a wonderful natural loaf with the best flour, slow risen and baked to perfection, for less than half of the cost of buying a comparable loaf in the shops.

So is it truly easy to make bread? Yes, simplicity itself. Combine store-cupboard ingredients – flour, yeast and salt, add water and oil – then wait, and in about two hours you have a golden fragrant loaf. You need no special equipment – hands and an oven are fine. I am not a fan of bread machines; I have always felt that money spent on excess kitchen equipment would have been better spent on shoes. Bread machines these days make perfectly adequate bread, but why would adequate be enough when you can make splendid bread by hand?

If you have a free-standing mixer with a dough hook then now is the time to use it, but even though I do have one, I often make the dough by hand. It's very soothing kneading bread; you can think about life, listen to the Archers, or simply work out any stress and anxiety you feel on the dough.

Kneading is easy, as, basically, all you are doing is stretching the dough. There is no right or wrong way, you just need to fold the raw mixture until it becomes smooth and elastic, not until your arms ache. I've been making bread for twenty years, and have never worked up a sweat when kneading. And whilst it is perfectly OK to slap the dough down and stretch it vigorously, it's not strictly necessary.

Bread dough is wonderfully versatile and a plain batch can be flavoured in many different ways. One obvious thing to do is to knead in some chopped nuts, seeds or herbs. Crushed whole spices, too, make a lovely addition. Crisp fried shallots can be kneaded into a wholemeal (whole-wheat) bread dough to make delicious onion bread, especially when shaped and baked as rolls, and chocolate chips kneaded into white bread dough make lovely breakfast rolls. The point to consider here is that the added ingredient must not be too wet. So onions sweated and then fried crisp, dried pears or tomatoes rather than fresh, hard cheese rather than soft. Once you have bread-making at your fingertips you will be able to be more adventurous and experiment for yourself.

Bread dough is amazingly long suffering, and will sit quite happily for three or four days in the fridge before you bake it. The dough freezes well, too, and so you can make a batch of plain dough and add different extras or flavours to it when thawed.

There are many different shapes you can make the bread into, the simplest being an oval loaf, baked either on a baking sheet or in a loaf tin. You don't need special tins as you can easily bake your loaf on a baking sheet or even in a roasting tin. Cake tins are excellent for making rolls tucked closely in and baked together ready to be pulled apart at the table. I have a loose-bottomed springform tin I use when baking stuffed bread. I make this by rolling the dough out to a rectangle and then spreading on a variety of fillings: olive tapenade, sun-dried tomato paste, pesto, brown sugar, butter and chopped pecans. I then roll this up with the filling inside, cut it into slices, and pack these, cut-side uppermost, into the tin before baking until golden.

Once you've managed your first loaf there will be no stopping you, as all the varieties of bread are at your fingertips. Why not make Parmesan bread sticks, olive bread, cinnamon buns...? With no costly equipment, no expensive ingredients and a guaranteed wow factor, now is the right time to get into the kitchen and start baking.

Bread-making Ingredients

The list is really quite short and all these ingredients will be available from your local shops or supermarkets.

Flour

Bread is traditionally made with wheat flour. This flour is high in gluten, the protein that gives bread its texture, and it is this gluten that is stretched during kneading. The more the dough is kneaded the finer the crumb, so for a bread like ciabatta, the dough isn't kneaded but beaten with a spoon to give the holey, open texture.

Bread flour is often labelled as such, or as strong flour. Essentially, this is a flour high in the looked-for wheat gluten. Bread flour can be white, wholemeal (whole-wheat) or a ready created mix such as granary, which is a brand and is white flour with whole grains already incorporated.

When buying flour, look for good quality. No doubt you will find many local mills that grind excellent flours, and several well-known brands, readily available from supermarkets, are excellent. For more economy, supermarket own-brands are just fine.

Rye flour is also often used in bread-making. The flour is lower in gluten than wheat, and so I often combine it with wheat flour to make the finished loaf lighter.

If you want to make an enriched yeast dough, say for brioche or rum baba, then I would use a regular plain (all-purpose) flour.

Yeast

Yeast is what gives bread its lightness and lift. Yeast is a living organism that feeds on the starch in the flour. As the yeast grows, it gives off carbon dioxide and these bubbles lift the strands of gluten in the dough. Yeast likes a warm damp environment, so bread should be made with warm water and put to rise in a warm place. A room you are comfortable in is just fine.

Fresh yeast

I prefer to work with fresh yeast which I buy from my local baker. Supermarkets with bakeries will also often supply you with fresh yeast. Fresh yeast keeps for about ten days if stored closely wrapped in the fridge. It freezes well, but you need to divide it into small pieces first. I use a walnut-in-its-shell-size piece for most baking, so I freeze these amounts wrapped in clingfilm (plastic wrap). Have a look at the basic bread recipe for how to use.

Dried yeast

Dried yeast comes in two forms: granular and instant. Of the two, I prefer granular, which comes in tins that you spoon the yeast from. The basic bread recipe will tell you how to use this.

Salt

Salt is essential in the bread-making process as it not only adds flavour but works to check the action of the yeast. In home baking this is not of the utmost importance, but it is as well to remember that too much salt will stop the yeast working fully. Allow about 1 dessertspoon of salt to 500g/18oz/5 cups flour and 1 tablespoon yeast.

Fat

Bread doesn't need fat, but oils and butter add flavour, and increase the keeping qualities of the loaves. I prefer to use extra virgin olive oil or butter, depending on which recipe I'm making.

❦❧

I've concentrated above on bread, but this chapter also includes other goodies, such as a cake – the famous lardy cake – and hot cross buns, both of which are made with a yeast dough. The chapter is also devoted to pastries, and pastry-making is another of those old-fashioned skills which is in danger of being lost. I give a few recipes for basic pastries, and what can be made from them, and I write about the rules and techniques on pages 68–69.

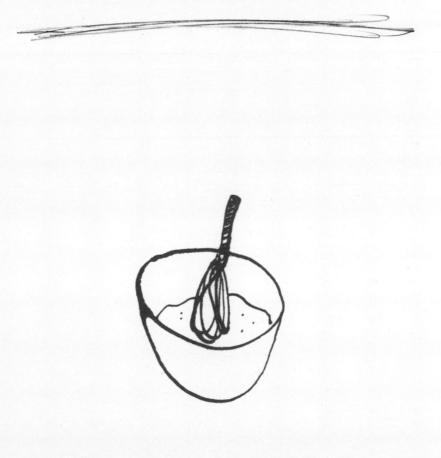

Basic Bread Recipe

This is where you begin. The simplest of loaves and, if this is the first time you have made bread, the most magical. Bread needs a little time and a few ingredients; once you have mastered this recipe, you can make almost any bread you desire.

Let's start with the yeast. If you are using fresh yeast, crumble it into a small bowl and add the honey or sugar. Using a wooden spoon, mix the two together until you have a liquid. If you look closely you will see the yeast starting to bubble almost at once, so eager is it to work. Add the tepid water and stir.

If you are using dried granular yeast, mix the honey/sugar into the tepid water then, using a fork, whisk in the yeast. The yeast won't dissolve all at once but this is not important.

Take about 2 tablespoons of the measured flour and sprinkle it on the surface of whichever yeast mixture you are using. There is no need to mix this in. Leave this 'sponge' in a warm place for about 10–15 minutes until it is really frothy. The yeast will have started to grow and you can see the bubbles forming.

Put the flour into a large bowl, and make a well in the centre. Add the salt to the flour and then pour in the yeast mixture plus half the oil or melted butter. Mix together to form a rough dough. I use only one hand to do this. It's quite simple to get into this habit, and you then always have the other hand clean to answer the phone or lift a glass.

> **Makes 1 loaf**
>
> 1 walnut-sized piece fresh yeast *or* 1 scant tablespoon dried granular yeast
> 1 teaspoon clear honey or unrefined sugar
> 300ml/10fl oz/1¼ cups hand-hot water, about 40°C/100°F
> 500g/18oz/5 cups strong white (bread) flour
> 1 teaspoon fine sea salt
> 4 tablespoons fruity olive oil, melted butter or vegetable oil

Once you have a rough ball of dough, tap the contents of the bowl on to a board. Now you must knead the dough until it is smooth and elastic. This stretches the gluten to give an evenly risen loaf. Look at the rough dough – it will look stringy. This is the gluten, and it is this you will be stretching.

There is no wrong way to do this. I knead by turning and folding the dough, the stretch coming on the fold. Continue to turn and fold the dough until it changes in character and becomes smooth and springy when lightly pressed. This takes about 5–8 minutes.

As flour is affected by the weather, you may need to add a little more to your dough if it seems too sticky to knead. Be warned, though – as the dough is kneaded the flour expands and takes up the water, so add only the lightest 'talcum' dusting of extra flour if really necessary, bearing in mind the maxim 'the wetter the dough, the better the bread'.

Now pour the remaining oil or butter in the recipe into your reserved mixing bowl (there is no need to wash it), and put in the ball of dough. Roll it in the oil/butter until the outer surface is covered, but do not mix it in.

Cover the bowl with a dry cloth and put the dough to rise in a warm place if you want to continue making the loaf, or cover with clingfilm (plastic wrap) and place in the fridge if you wish to store it for later.

Once the dough has doubled in size – which will take about 1 hour in a warm room – you are ready to continue.

Knock back the dough – I like to punch it! Take it from the bowl and then knead it once more until the oil has been incorporated into the dough.

You are now ready to shape your loaf. Either roll it into an oblong, tucking the ends in, and place in a 1kg/2¼lb loaf tin, or simply shape it into a round and place on a greased baking sheet.

Brush the top with a beaten egg glaze or scatter over a little extra flour and leave once more to rise. This rising will take less time, about 45 minutes in a warm room.

Meanwhile, preheat the oven to 200°C/400°F/Gas Mark 6.

Place the bread in the centre of the oven and bake until well risen and golden brown, about 20–25 minutes. The loaf will sound hollow when tapped on the base. If you are unsure if the bread is cooked, err on the well-done side and give it an extra 5 minutes

Turn the bread out on to a wire cooling rack. When cold, eat and enjoy.

Yeast-based Sourdough Starter

Makes about 500ml/18fl oz

First stage
1½ teaspoons dried yeast
140g/5oz/scant 1½ cups plain
    (all-purpose) flour
225ml/8fl oz/1 cup warm water

Second stage
140g/5oz/scant 1½ cups plain
    (all-purpose) flour
225ml/8fl oz/1 cup milk
60g/2¼oz/⅓ cup caster (superfine) sugar

This starter I have found to be fail-safe and it keeps well. It is based on a recipe from the Amish communities in North America, who are famed for their baking skills. Sourdoughs are, for many, the gold standard of bread-making, as the flavour and rise of the bread are developed slowly, giving a much improved texture and taste. As it's not always possible to have a bowl of dough fermenting for up to seven days, using a 'starter' gives you all the flavour and some of the texture of a long-risen loaf.

My starter is fourteen years old at least, and while it sometimes looks a little scary, it should, when stirred, be smooth and smell like yoghurt. Even if you don't use the starter for a couple of weeks it will need the occasional feed.

Mix the first-stage ingredients together in a glass, china or plastic bowl. Cover and leave in a warm place for three days, stirring daily. By this time the mixture should be frothy and have a sour smell.

Now add the second-stage ingredients, and stir well. Don't worry if the mixture looks a little lumpy. Cover and place in the fridge. Stir again each day and, after 5 days, the starter is ready to use.

To keep this starter going, add 2 tablespoons each of flour and milk and a teaspoon of sugar each time you take 4 tablespoons of starter out.

As rye flour contains little gluten – the very stuff that makes bread bread – I mix it with wheat flour for a lighter loaf. This bread makes lovely toast, which I particularly enjoy with butter and honey. Adding a few crushed caraway seeds turns this into an eastern European loaf, delicious with smoked fish.

In a bowl, cream the fresh yeast together with the honey, using a wooden spoon, then add the water and mix. (If using dried yeast, mix the honey into the water and sprinkle on the dried yeast. Stir and continue as with fresh.) Sprinkle on a tablespoon of the white flour and leave to stand for 15 minutes or until frothy. Add the sourdough starter.

Put the two flours into another bowl, and mix in the salt. Add the yeast mixture. Work it together to give a ball of dough, using your hands, then turn on to a board and knead for 5–8 minutes or until the dough is smooth and elastic. Return to an oiled bowl, cover with a damp cloth and put in a warm spot to rise.

Once the dough has doubled in size, about 1 hour, knock it back and knead lightly. Shape into two loaves – I find a rough oval or round works well. Using your sharpest knife, cut a couple of diagonal slashes through the top of each loaf and place on a lightly floured baking sheet. Leave until doubled in size once more, about another 30 minutes, depending on the warmth of the room.

Preheat oven to 200°C/400°F/Gas Mark 6.

Bake in the preheated oven for 25–30 minutes or until golden brown and hollow when tapped. Cool before serving.

Sourdough Rye Bread

Makes 2 loaves

1 walnut-sized piece of fresh yeast *or* 1 scant tablespoon dried yeast
½ teaspoon clear honey
400ml/14fl oz/1¾ cups warm water
500g/18oz/5 cups strong white (bread) flour
3 tablespoons sourdough starter (see page 58)
300g/10½oz/3¼ cups rye flour
1 teaspoon fine sea salt
1 tablespoon olive oil

To achieve the traditional loaf shape, you can lightly flour a small oval basket and use this as a mould during the second rising. Carefully tip the risen loaf onto a tray and allow an extra 5 minutes to rest before baking.

Sourdough Ciabatta

Makes 4 loaves

1½ teaspoons dried yeast

120ml/4fl oz/½ cup warm water

1 tablespoon fine sea salt

900g/2lb/9 cups organic plain (all-purpose)
   flour, plus extra for dusting

2 tablespoons sourdough starter
   (see page 58)

600ml/1 pint warm water

2–3 tablespoons olive oil

*Ciabatta is surely one of our most loved
Italian breads. Characterized by its open
crumb and holey texture, this bread is the
perfect addition to any antipasto plate.
I love to serve it with pasta, and even split
the loaves and top the pieces like pizza
before popping them to bake in the oven
for about 10 minutes.*

*This is the best recipe for ciabatta I have
tried. The dough is very sticky, so use a
light touch and handle as little as possible.*

Mix the yeast with the 120ml/4fl oz/½ cup
warm water and leave to sit for 15 minutes
in a warm place.

In a large bowl, mix the salt thoroughly
into the flour and then add the yeast and
its water, the sourdough starter and, a little
at a time, the 600ml/1 pint/2 cups warm
water. The dough will be very sticky, but
don't worry. You will not be able to knead
this in the traditional fashion, so beat the
mix with your hand or a wooden spoon
until the flour is combined and the dough
looks a little stringy.

Scrape the dough into a ball and, leaving
it in the bowl, drizzle over the oil, turning
the ball of dough so that the surface is
oiled. Cover the bowl with clingfilm (plastic
wrap) and set in a warm place to rise for
about 2 hours, or until doubled in size.

Flour a large board heavily. Tip the
dough from the bowl, scraping it out if
necessary. Using a knife, cut the dough into
four pieces and, handling it gently, separate
the dough, laying each piece in the flour.
Leave for 10 minutes then pick up the
dough, stretching each piece gently into an
oblong shape. Invert on to greased baking
sheets. The top of the bread will be very
floury. You should have four loaves, each
about 30 x 10cm/12 x 4in. Cover loosely
with clingfilm and leave to rise for a
further 40–60 minutes or until doubled in
size. The dough should spring back when
lightly pressed with your finger, leaving
only a slight indentation.

Meanwhile, preheat the oven to 230ºC/
450ºF/Gas Mark 8 for at least 30 minutes
before baking the bread. Using a spray
bottle mist the bread with water and
place in the preheated oven. Turn the
temperature down to 200ºC/400ºF/
Gas Mark 6 and bake the bread for
25–30 minutes or until crusty and hollow
when tapped.

Remove from the oven and tip on to
a wire cooling rack.

I usually make this bread with a glut of fresh ripe tomatoes. Simply chop enough to give you a rough 500ml/18fl oz/2¼ cups, sprinkle on the salt and oil and leave for a few hours for the tomatoes to sweat.

Whilst this bread looks very good, like a handsome man it can disappoint, so adding some chopped dried tomatoes beefs up the flavour. I would use about 55–85g/ 2–3oz/⅓–½ cup chopped sun-dried or sun-blush tomatoes. Other herbs can replace the basil: thyme and rosemary work well, and I have even added some crumbled feta cheese on occasions...

In this recipe, I've not started the yeast separately as we are not adding any water. Fresh yeast works best here, but dried will be just fine – it might take another 30 minutes to achieve the first rise.

Pile the flour on to your work surface and make a well in the centre. Tip in the tomatoes and basil. Sprinkle on the yeast, adding the salt and oil if not already in.

Mix everything together, kneading for about 10 minutes. The water from the tomatoes will gradually take up all the flour. You are looking for a moist dough. Place in an oiled bowl and allow to double in size, about 1 hour in a warm room.

Knock back the dough, and shape into a loaf or about a dozen rolls. Place on an oiled baking sheet and allow to double in size once more. This time the rise should be quicker, about 30–45 minutes.

Preheat the oven to 200ºC/400ºF/Gas Mark 6.

Bake the loaf in the preheated oven for 25–35 minutes, or until a hollow sound is heard when the base is tapped. The rolls should take about 15–20 minutes. Remove, and allow to cool before using.

Tomato & Basil Bread

Makes 1 loaf or 12 rolls

600g/1lb 5oz/scant 7 cups white (bread) flour

1 x 400g/14oz tin chopped tomatoes (*or* approx. 500ml/18fl oz/2¼ cups chopped fresh tomatoes)

a good handful of fresh basil leaves, finely sliced

1 walnut-sized piece of fresh yeast *or* a scant tablespoon dried yeast

1 tablespoon fine sea salt

4 tablespoons olive oil

Cherry tomatoes have a lovely flavour but the ratio of skin to flesh is too high for this recipe. Use a larger variety of fruiting tomatoes.

Lardy Cake

Makes 1 loaf/cake

175–340g/6–12oz/¾–1½ cups lard
  (see below), softened
175g/6oz/scant 1 cup caster (superfine)
  sugar
225g/8oz/1½ cups mixed dried fruit

Basic bread recipe
1 walnut-sized piece of fresh yeast
  or a scant tablespoon dried yeast
½ teaspoon clear honey
300ml/10fl oz/1¼ cups hand-hot water
1 teaspoon fine sea salt
500g/18oz/5 cups strong white (bread)
  flour
4 tablespoons fruity olive oil

The bread recipe given here you can use by itself to make a basic bread. Once mastered, you can make almost any bread you desire, such as the following lardy cake.

This Wiltshire tradition is as delicious as it is packed with fat and sugar. It is definitely a special treat, but well worth the making.

As this makes quite a large cake, I often freeze half for later. I have offered a variable weight of lard so that you can decide on the richness of the finished loaf. However, I would suggest you use the larger amount and simply eat smaller pieces...

Make the bread dough first. Cream the yeast with the honey, add the water and mix. Sprinkle on a tablespoon of the flour and leave to stand for 15 minutes or until frothy.

In a large bowl, mix the salt into the flour then add the yeast mixture and the olive oil. Work together to give a ball of dough then turn this on to a board and knead for 5–8 minutes or until the dough is smooth and elastic.

Return to an oiled bowl, cover with a damp cloth and put in a warm spot to rise.

Once the dough has doubled in size, about 1 hour, knock it back and knead lightly. On a floured board, roll it into a rectangle about 35 x 29cm/14 x 11½in. Spread two-thirds of the dough nearest to you with the lard, and sprinkle with the sugar and fruit. Then, as if making puff pastry, turn the top third down and the bottom third up, press to seal the edges, give the dough a quarter turn and roll to a rectangle.

Repeat the folding and rolling twice more, then roll the dough out to fit a deep 30 x 20cm/12 x 8in baking tin. Put the dough in the tin in a warm place and leave to rise until doubled in size, about 1 hour.

Preheat the oven to 220ºC/425ºF/Gas Mark 7. Bake the cake in the preheated oven for about 45 minutes until risen and golden brown. When you take the cake from the oven it will be swimming in fat.

Carefully turn the cake over in the tin, sprinkle with a little caster (superfine) sugar and allow to cool. The dough will absorb the fat.

Remove from the tin when cold and cut into thin slices. Eat it with large cups of tea or coffee. It makes a wonderful addition to a picnic, and is just the thing after a day on the beach. This lardy cake freezes well.

Hot Cross Buns

Makes 18 buns

175g/6oz/1¾ cups wholemeal (whole-
    wheat) flour
300g/10½oz/2⅓ cups strong white (bread)
    flour
1 teaspoon fine sea salt
3 teaspoons mixed spice
55g/2oz/scant ⅓ cup light muscovado
    sugar
35g/1¼oz/scant ¼ cup fresh yeast
1 tablespoon clear honey
225ml/8fl oz/16 cups warm water
1 egg
55g/2oz/½ stick butter, melted
2 tablespoons sourdough starter (optional)
150g/5½oz/1 cup each of sultanas and
    candied mixed peel
finely grated zest of 1 lemon

To finish

2 tablespoons plain (all-purpose) flour,
    mixed to a wettish paste with 1–2 table-
    spoons water (pastry for the crosses)
1 egg, beaten
2 tablespoons caster (superfine) sugar
2 tablespoons boiling water

Mix the flours, salt, spice and sugar in a large bowl.

In a small bowl, cream the yeast with the honey until it becomes liquid. Pour in the warm water and add about a tablespoon of the flour mix. Stir well and then leave in a warm place for about 10 minutes or until frothy.

Once the yeast is bubbling add it, plus the egg and melted butter, to the flour. The sourdough starter should be added now too, if used. Mix the ingredients well, beating with a wooden spoon. Beat in the fruit and zest then cover the bowl and put it in a warm place. Leave the dough until it has at least doubled in size, which may take about 2 hours. Do not rush this rising, as the lightness of the end result depends on enough time being allowed for the dough to prove thoroughly.

Tip or scrape the dough out on to a floured board and cut into 18 pieces. Knead each one into a bun shape and place on greased baking sheets.

Cover with a damp cloth and again put to rise in a warm place. The dough should double in size again, but this time the rising will be shorter, about 20–30 minutes.

When you put the buns to rise, switch the oven on to 220°C/425°F/Gas Mark 7 and allow to heat.

Using the beaten egg, brush the top of each bun. Then, either using a piping bag or a spoon, drizzle the flour/water mix over the buns to form a cross.

Bake the buns in the preheated oven for 20–25 minutes or until golden brown.

Mix the caster (superfine) sugar with the water to make a sugar glaze, stirring until dissolved. Remove the buns from the oven and at once brush with the glaze. Allow to cool on a rack.

I love to make my own breads, and like to continue baking traditions, so always make at least one batch of these buns at Easter. The dough is very soft so you won't be able to knead it in the usual way, but the resulting buns are wonderfully light and fragrant. If you have any sourdough starter in the fridge, add 2 tablespoons to the dough along with the yeast.

Pastry

Making pastry can seem a little daunting. Those who do it with ease often seem to create a mystery around pastry. 'Do you have cold hands?' they ask, 'Have you a light touch?' I can say no to both these questions but still make good pastry, for two reasons: firstly, I understand how pastry works, and, secondly, I have a food processor!

The essence of pastry is that fat is mixed with flour and then liquid added. Its origins were to make a tough-resistant pie crust or 'coffin' in which to bake the smaller pieces of meat unsuitable for spit roasting. Once the pie was opened, the contents were eaten and the pastry discarded.

We have all eaten pastry like that, but a few pointers will make you a perfect pastry cook.

❖ The higher the ratio of fat to flour, the more melting the pastry, but the more difficult it is to handle.

❖ The more water you add to the dough, the more the pastry will shrink but the flakier it will be.

❖ The more you knead the dough, working the gluten in the flour, the tougher the pastry will become.

❖ Adding lard to pastry gives a crisper finish.

❖ Adding sugar to pastry gives a biscuit-like finish.

❖ Pastry made with butter is delicious – not really a pointer, just a fact!

❖ Chilling pastry makes it much easier to handle.

❖ Don't over-flour your board, as all that extra flour will be rolled into the pastry, ruining your carefully weighed mix.

Each and every one of these facts can be used to good effect. So if you want a flaky pastry to wrap a samosa, you will need one with more water but also one that has been kneaded a little to make it tough enough to hold the filling.

I always use a food processor to rub the fat into the flour. Use short bursts of power. Once the mix looks like breadcrumbs or ground almonds, tip it into a large mixing bowl and continue by hand. The point of this is not to let the fat melt and so be absorbed by the flour. This is where the cold hands and light touch come into play.

I also always use salted butter when making pastry, but the choice there is yours.

Standard Shortcrust Pastry

Makes approx. 450g/1lb

115g/4oz/1 stick cold butter, cut into
    small pieces
225g/8oz/2⅓ cups plain (all-purpose)
    flour
1 egg yolk
approx. 2 tablespoons iced water

*This is the one to use for mince pies, jam
tarts, quiches, pasties and simple pies.*

Using a food processor or your fingertips,
rub the butter into the flour until the
mixture resembles breadcrumbs. Now,
using the blade of a knife, add the egg
yolk and enough cold water to form a
stiff dough.

 Pull the dough together, kneading very
lightly for about 5 seconds. It just needs to
become a smoothish ball, then press into
a disc shape.

 Wrap in clingfilm (plastic wrap) and
chill for 30 minutes.

Easy Sweet Pastry

Makes 450g/1lb

140g/5oz/1¼ sticks butter, softened
1 egg
55g/2oz/scant ⅓ cup caster
    (superfine) sugar
a pinch of fine sea salt
225g/8oz/scant 2⅓ cups plain
    (all-purpose) flour

*This is the world's simplest sweet pastry
recipe. Don't be put off by the initial look
of the mixture, things get better!*

In a large bowl and using a balloon whisk,
beat the butter and egg together. Add the
sugar and salt and continue beating until
the mixture is relatively smooth. Now add
the flour and mix this in well.

 Knead together lightly, dusting your
hands with a little extra flour if necessary.

 Wrap in clingfilm (plastic wrap) and
chill for at least 30 minutes before using
to line tart or pie tins.

Rough Puff Pastry

Makes approx. 450g/1lb

225g/8oz/scant 2⅓ cups plain
   (all-purpose) flour
½ teaspoon fine sea salt
175g/6oz/1½ sticks butter
2–3 tablespoons cold water

I buy frozen puff pastry, but on occasions like to make rough puff at home.

Sift the flour and salt into a bowl. Divide the butter into three equal parts and, with your fingers rub one part of it into the flour. When the mixture resembles coarse crumbs, add sufficient water to form a firmish dough. The dough should not be sticky.

Place the dough on a lightly floured board and roll out to give a strip 30 x 10cm/ 12 x 4in. Take one part of the remaining butter and, cutting small pieces, dab these over two-thirds of the surface of the pastry. Fold the bottom third up then the top third down, press to seal the edges and chill for 20 minutes.

Placing the pressed edges horizontal to you, roll the dough to give a strip 30 x 10cm/ 12 x 4in. Repeat the process with the remaining butter. Fold, seal, chill and roll once more.

Wrap in clingfilm (plastic wrap) and chill until needed.

Pastry for Samosas, Empañadas and Pasties

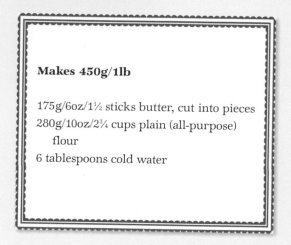

Makes 450g/1lb

175g/6oz/1½ sticks butter, cut into pieces
280g/10oz/2¾ cups plain (all-purpose)
   flour
6 tablespoons cold water

This pastry is quite elastic but can be tricky to handle. Chill in two parts, using one before removing the second from the fridge.

Rub the butter into the flour until the mixture resembles coarse breadcrumbs, either with your fingers or in a food processor. Tip into a large bowl and then add the water, stirring with the blade of a knife. Knead for about 30 seconds until the dough is smooth.

Divide the pastry into two discs, wrap in clingfilm (plastic wrap) and chill for 30 minutes.

Hot-water Crust Pastry

This pastry is the one that goes against everything I've said before! Here, the fat is melted, the flour beaten in, and the dough used warm. If, the first time you roll it, it is too fragile to move, simple re-form the ball and wait a few moments then try again.

This pastry is most commonly used for raised pies, either pork, game or veal and ham.

Sift the flour with the salt into a large bowl and make a well in the centre.

Put the milk, water and lard into a saucepan and heat until the lard melts. Bring the mixture to the boil and then pour into the well in the flour. Beat the mixture with a wooden spoon until you have a smooth dough.

Turn on to a lightly floured board and as soon as the dough is cool enough to touch, knead lightly. Return to the bowl and cover with a folded towel to keep warm. Make the pastry just before you need it. It should be used just warm, as it is very difficult to roll out once cold.

Makes 700g/1lb 9oz, enough for a large 20cm/8in pork or game pie

450g/1lb/4½ cups plain (all-purpose) flour
1 teaspoon fine sea salt
120ml/4fl oz/½ cup each of milk and
    water
175g/6oz/¾ cup lard

Choux Pastry

*Another 'hot' pastry, this one is
wonderfully useful. Think profiteroles,
choux buns and beignets. Choux is so much
simpler than it sounds – the only thing
to watch carefully for is that the mixture
doesn't become too soft to pipe (it may be
necessary to hold back a little of the egg).
You're looking for a smooth glossy mixture
that just holds its shape when dropped
from the spoon. Don't panic, though, if you
feel you've gone too far. Simply spoon the
choux on to the baking sheet and follow the
cooking instructions, adding a couple of
extra minutes' cooking time.*

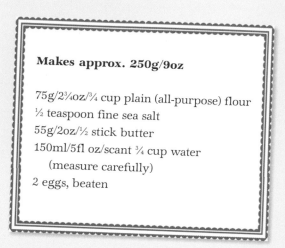

Makes approx. 250g/9oz

75g/2¾oz/¾ cup plain (all-purpose) flour
½ teaspoon fine sea salt
55g/2oz/½ stick butter
150ml/5fl oz/scant ¾ cup water
   (measure carefully)
2 eggs, beaten

Sift the flour and salt together on to a plate.

Place the butter and water in a medium
non-stick saucepan and heat until the
butter has dissolved. Now bring the
mixture to the boil and, when boiling, tip
in the salted flour, all in one go. Turn off
the heat, and beat well with a wooden
spoon until smooth. The mixture should
form a ball in the saucepan, leaving the
sides clean. (You could also put the mixture
in a food processor. Use short bursts of
power and don't over-process.)

Allow to cool for about 5 minutes.
Meanwhile, preheat the oven to 200ºC/
400ºF/Gas Mark 6.

Beat the egg into the dough, a little at
a time, to give a smooth glossy paste that
holds its shape (see above).

Pipe or spoon the choux pastry on to a
damp baking sheet to give small walnut-
sized balls, or pipe into eclairs – these
could be tiny, say 5cm/2in, or full-sized
10cm/4in ones.

Place in the preheated oven for
10 minutes, then turn down the heat to
190ºC/375ºF/Gas Mark 5, and cook for

a further 10–15 minutes, or until the puffs
are golden brown.

Remove from the oven, pierce with a
knife to let the steam out and return to the
oven for about 5 minutes to crisp.

Cool on a rack before filling with
whipped cream or crème pâtissière. Eclairs
can be dipped in melted chocolate or coffee
glacé icing to finish.

Choux pastry flaunts all the rules of pastry-making, as cool hands and a light touch are not needed. You will have to beat the eggs into the flour mix quite vigorously, but, should you find this a chore, just tip the mix into a food processor or use an electric whisk.

These beignets freeze very well and, after defrosting, can be reheated in a medium oven for 10 minutes.

Make the dough as described on page 72. When the mixture is stiff and glossy, beat in the remaining ingredients. This dough can be made up to an hour before cooking. Cover it well.

When you are ready to cook the beignets, heat about 2.5cm/1in of oil in a large pan and fry dessertspoons of the mixture a few at a time, turning once until they are golden brown and puffed (3–4 minutes). Continue until all the mixture is used, keeping the cooked beignets warm.

Serve at once, sprinkled with a mixture of grated Parmesan, paprika and pepper, accompanied by a side salad.

Tuna Beignets

Makes approx. 20 puffs

1 quantity choux pastry (see page 72)
175g/6oz tinned tuna, drained and flaked
35g/1¼oz/scant ¼ cup Parmesan cheese, freshly grated
1 teaspoon Dijon mustard
½ teaspoon paprika
freshly ground black pepper

To cook and serve
vegetable oil, for frying
freshly grated Parmesan cheese, paprika and freshly ground black pepper

I have used tuna here, but tiny cubes of cheese, salami or sun-dried tomato also make excellent beignets.

Cheese Straws

Makes approx. 40

225g/8oz/2 sticks cold butter
350g/12oz/scant 3½ cups plain
    (all-purpose) flour
fine sea salt
2 egg yolks
225g/8oz/1¼ cups Cheddar cheese, grated
about 2–3 tablespoons cold water

To finish
1 egg, beaten
freshly grated Parmesan cheese
celery, cumin or fennel seeds, crushed

I think home-made cheese straws are in a different league from shop-bought ones. Two factors decide this: the quality of the cheese, and the quantity. I use extra-mature (sharp) Cheddar as I like a bite to my cheese, but don't cut back on the amount of cheese if you prefer a milder cheese taste, just cut back on the strength of the Cheddar you use.

If you like, you can spread a layer of mustard over the pastry before adding the first layer of cheese.

In a large bowl, rub the butter into the flour and salt, then add the egg yolks, 55g/2oz/ ½ cup of the cheese and enough cold water to form a stiff dough. Wrap in clingfilm (plastic wrap) and chill for 30 minutes.

Form the dough into an oblong and roll out very thinly on a board.

Sprinkle about half the remaining cheese over two-thirds of the dough, bring the unsprinkled part over half the sprinkled part in such a way as to trap air, then bring the remaining third over to make three layers. Press the open edges together lightly. Turn with the folds to the left-hand side. (This is the same technique you use for puff pastry.) Roll out again into an oblong and repeat the sprinkling of the cheese and folding of the dough.

Preheat oven to 220ºC/425ºF/Gas Mark 7.

Roll out to 1cm/½in thick and trim the edges. Cut into strips 5cm/2in long and then into wafers 1cm/½in wide. Place on a baking sheet and brush with beaten egg. Now scatter over some Parmesan and a few crushed seeds.

Bake the cheese straws in the preheated oven for 10–12 minutes, or until golden brown. Using a spatula, remove to a wire rack and leave to cool.

Store for up to a month in an airtight tin, refreshing for 5 minutes in a hot oven before serving.

Game Pie

Serves 8–10

1 quantity hot-water crust pastry (page 71)
lard, for greasing
1 egg, beaten, to glaze

Filling
85g/3oz/¾ stick butter
3 large shallots, peeled and chopped
1 plump garlic clove, peeled and crushed
450g/1lb wild rabbit meat (i.e. the meat
    from 1 large or 2 small rabbits), or
    young venison
approx. 225g/8oz thinly cut streaky
    bacon, rinded
450g/1lb fat belly of pork, boned and
    rind removed
1 teaspoon fresh thyme leaves
1 teaspoon chopped fresh sage leaves
1 teaspoon juniper berries, crushed
2 tablespoons brandy
coarse sea salt and freshly ground black
    pepper
1 tablespoon green peppercorns
breast meat of 1 pheasant or 2 partridges

*Here is my favourite pie recipe. You can use
a mixture of different game meats.*

*When making baked pies or terrines it is
very important that the seasoning is right
before they go into the oven. Once cooked,
this cannot be changed. My solution is to fry
small patties of the meat, tasting them until
I think the seasoning is correct. Remember
that meat must taste over-seasoned when
hot, as cold numbs the flavour.*

First make the pastry as described on
page 71. Put in a bowl and cover with a
folded towel to keep warm. To make the
filling, melt the butter then gently fry
the shallot and garlic until soft, about
5–7 minutes. Allow to cool.

Mince the rabbit (or venison), bacon and
pork together twice using the finest blade
of the mincer. Place the meat in a large
bowl and add the herbs, crushed juniper
berries, the butter, shallot and garlic
mixture, the brandy, salt and pepper. Mix
the farce well then fry a small piece to taste.
Correct seasoning if necessary and now stir
in the green peppercorns.

Generously grease a loose-bottomed 20 x
7.5cm/8 x 3in round cake tin with lard, and
line with greaseproof (waxed) paper.

Break off two-thirds of the dough and
roll to give a circle large enough to line the
whole tin. Once you have placed the pastry
in the tin, press in half the filling. Lay strips
of pheasant or partridge breast meat over
the stuffing, then press on the remaining
mixture. Roll out the remaining pastry to
form a top and cover the pie, sealing and
crimping the edges. Cut a steam vent in the
middle, decorate with leaves rolled from the
pastry trimmings, and brush the surface
with egg glaze. Chill for 30 minutes.

Preheat the oven to 200°C/400°F/Gas
Mark 6. Bake the pie in the preheated oven
for 20 minutes then turn the heat down to
180°C/350°F/Gas Mark 4 and continue to
cook the pie for a further 2 hours.

Remove from the oven, cool for 5 minutes,
then remove the pie from the tin and allow
to cool completely. If you wish, you could
pour a little warm jellied chicken stock in
through the steam vent.

Serve cold, with pickles or chutney. Pies
like these are a wonderful addition to a cold
collation, and make great winter picnic food.

Raised Pork Pie

Serves 8–10

1 quantity hot-water crust pastry (see page 71)
lard, for greasing
1 egg, to glaze

Filling
3 shallots, peeled and chopped
olive oil
800g/1¾lb trimmed lean pork
115g/4oz streaky bacon, rinded
4–5 fresh sage leaves, torn
ground mace and allspice
sea salt and freshly ground black pepper

A handsome pie and good enough to grace any table. I grew up in Lincolnshire where eating pork pie is obligatory, and I love it. No Christmas feast can be without one standing centre stage. If I have weekend visitors, I make one (as that's breakfast sorted) and, naturally, meals on the hoof outside need pies.

First make the pastry as described on page 71. Put in a bowl and cover with a folded towel to keep warm.

For the filling, cook the shallots in a little oil until sweet and tender, about 5–7 minutes. Allow to cool.

Roughly dice the meat and rinded bacon then place in a food processor with the torn sage leaves, a good few pinches of mace and allspice and lots of salt and pepper. If you have an electric mincer, use this to prepare the farce. Whiz the mixture in short bursts until it is roughly chopped and well combined.

Mix in the shallots and fry a small ball of the meat so you may taste and correct the seasoning. Remember, when the meat is eaten hot the spices will taste stronger, so adjust as necessary.

Generously grease a loose-bottomed 20 x 7.5cm/8 x 3in round cake tin with lard, and line with greaseproof (waxed) paper.

Break off two-thirds of the dough and roll to give a circle large enough to line the whole tin. Once you have placed the pastry in the tin, press in all the filling. Roll out the remaining pastry to form a top and cover the pie, sealing and crimping the edges. Cut a steam vent in the middle, decorate with leaves rolled from the trimmings, and brush the surface with egg glaze. Chill for 30 minutes.

Preheat the oven to 200ºC/400ºF/ Gas Mark 6. Bake the pie as described on page 76. Cool in a similar way, and you could also pour in a little warm jellied chicken stock through the steam vent.

Steak & Kidney Pudding

Serves 6–8

1kg/2¼lb rump steak
500g/18oz veal or ox kidney, trimmed
2 tablespoons seasoned flour
1 large onion, peeled and chopped
90g/3¼oz/scant stick butter, plus extra,
    for greasing
600ml/1 pint/2 cups beef stock
250g/9oz/3¾ cups mushrooms, sliced
1 *bouquet garni*

Suet crust pastry
300g/10½oz/3 cups self-raising flour
1 level teaspoon baking powder
¼ teaspoon fine sea salt
freshly ground white pepper
¼ teaspoon fresh or dried thyme
150g/5½oz/¾ cup chopped suet
4–6 tablespoons cold water

This is one of those dishes that make grown men cry. The blueprint recipe can be used with a variety of fillings: a chicken and mushroom casserole could just as easily become chicken and mushroom pudding.

If you don't have a steamer, you will need a deep lidded saucepan. The pudding bowl should fit easily into the pan, standing on a trivet or an upturned saucer. The water should come halfway up the bowl. Cook the pudding over a low heat once the water has come up to a simmer. Have the lid on the pan, leaving a small vent for the steam, and top up with boiling water as the level falls.

Preheat the oven to 150ºC/300ºF/Gas Mark 2.

Cut the steak into neat 2cm/¾in pieces, and slice the kidney. Discard all the fat and skin from both meats. Sprinkle them with seasoned flour. Cook the onion until lightly browned in two-thirds of the butter, then add the meat and colour rapidly. Transfer the meat as it is browned to a casserole dish and add the stock.

Fry the mushrooms in the remaining butter and add them with the *bouquet garni* to the casserole. Cover with a lid and simmer in the preheated oven until the meat is almost cooked (1–1½ hours). Leave to cool.

For the crust, mix the dry ingredients in a bowl, stir in the cold water and mix to make a firm dough. Roll out into a circle on a lightly floured surface and cut off a quarter wedge for the lid.

Butter a 1.5 litre/2¾ pint pudding basin and press the large piece of pastry in to fit the basin, allowing 2.5cm/1in overhanging at the rim. Put the filling in (it should come no higher than 2.5cm/1in below the rim). Roll out the remaining suet crust to make a circle for the lid. Place on top of the bowl, and press the edges of the pastry together to make a firm seal. Cut some foil to make a circle larger all round than the top of the pudding basin. Fix it with your fingers so that it balloons above the pudding leaving it room to rise. Tie a string handle around the rim of the basin, so it can be easily lifted in and out of the steamer.

When the water is boiling in the lower part of the steamer, put the pudding in, cover with the lid, and leave for 1½-2 hours. Top up with boiling water when necessary. If you don't have a steamer, cook the pudding as described above.

Allow the pudding to sit for 15 minutes before turning out on to a large deep dish. Serve with mashed potato and a green vegetable such as cabbage.

CAKES
AND BISCUITS

Introduction

Every well-stocked pantry must contain several tins of home-made cakes and biscuits. A rather emphatic statement, but one for which I offer no apologies. Cakes and biscuits could never be described as an essential foodstuff, but they enhance life quite wonderfully.

I especially love home-made cake. Actually to be truthful, I love all cake. It's as simple as that. Maybe it's the sweetness, more likely it's the pure indulgence of it – cake being so completely unnecessary to nutrition – which makes it so very alluring. I even like looking at cake, standing at the window of those high-end bakeries where tiny but costly examples of the confectioner's art are displayed like jewels in a Bond Street window. But, life not being fair, I seldom actually eat cake, so having visitors makes for the perfect excuse to indulge myself.

Essential Cake Ingredients

Home-made cakes and biscuits need the very best ingredients.

Butter

I always choose butter as I think the taste incomparable. I also prefer lightly salted to unsalted butter as I find the flavour deeper, but that is a matter of personal taste.

Flours

I like to use flour from local mills, as there is a real link there with the community, but as long as you keep your flour in an airtight container, and make sure you don't store it longer than the recommended time given by the use-by date, all plain flour will work well. Plain (all-purpose) flour is a medium-gluten flour, with cake flour having even less gluten.

Self-raising flour is a mix of flour and baking powder. If you bake only occasionally, then I suggest you do as I do, and keep plain flour and baking powder separately, mixing them as and when you need. The proportions needed are usually on the baking powder container, but as a general rule for cake and scones, you need 1 teaspoon of baking powder for every 115g/4oz/1 cup flour. Muffins and soda breads might need a little more, but you must be a tad wary when using baking powder – put too much in a scone recipe, say, and the result will be well risen but bitter! If you find that your recipe seems a little heavy when baked, try adding an extra couple of spoonfuls of milk to loosen the mixture. This will help the baking powder to achieve its maximum effect.

The frequent home-baker may also want to keep some cornflour (cornstarch) in the pantry or larder. Adding a proportion of this gluten-free flour to biscuits will make the finished texture shorter, i.e. more crumbly. Whilst cornflour is free from gluten, it is not a sufficient substitute for wheat flour if you wish your baking to be gluten-free. Gluten-free flours, plain and self-raising, are readily available from supermarkets and health-food stores, and can be used with good results in these recipes. The cakes may not be as light, but they will taste excellent.

Buy baking powder in small containers and replace once the use-by date is past. It's not that the powder will spoil, but it will lose some of its potency and so the rise will be less assured.

Eggs

Use fresh eggs, free-range if you can find them. All the recipes in this book are made with large eggs.

One simple tip is to make sure both the eggs and butter are at room temperature before you start, if at all possible. The reason cake mixture curdles is that the liquid in the egg is either at a different temperature to the fat in the butter, or that both are very cold, and so the mix won't expand into an emulsion. Whilst the cake will still be both edible and delicious, the mixture will not rise as successfully.

Curdling is not a problem if you use a food processor to make cakes, as the speed of the blade creates the emulsion very efficiently. But, remember, if you use a food processor, be wary of over-working the flour once added. The gluten in the flour can be stretched by the whizzing of the blade, and this will make the cake tough. I find about five to six pulses is sufficient to mix the flour in successfully.

Sugar

I tend to use white caster (superfine) sugar for sponges and fancy biscuits but a raw, unrefined cane sugar for more wholesome cakes and biscuits. Look for the words 'unrefined' or 'raw sugar' on the label – some 'brown' sugar is simply white sugar sprayed with molasses.

When it comes to icing your cakes, you will need to buy icing (confectioners') sugar. I really think that the white rather than the unrefined icing sugar is best. Pale brown icing looks rather dull, and icing can never be a health food, so one might as well enjoy it...

Other Flavourings

I like to use vanilla extract or the newer vanilla bean paste. Vanilla comes from the vanilla orchid, in the long seedpods that grow only under perfect conditions. It is a rare and exotic plant, and so vanilla is costly. If you see something calling itself 'vanilla flavouring' at what seems like a real bargain price, it may well be synthetic vanillin, which, while not bad for you, is a poor imitation of the real thing.

Spices are best bought un-ground. Invest in a coffee grinder and keep it solely for spices. When you make a cup of coffee, you wouldn't go to the cupboard and fish around for some ground beans that are months, if not years, old. So why would you do it with spices? The added bonus of buying whole spices is that they keep their intense aroma far longer and you can use them whole, crushed or ground.

Whilst dried fruit is intended to keep well, it's best not to store it much more than a year. Older fruit becomes very dry and tough. It can, of course, be reconstituted by soaking in water, tea or even a little brandy!

Equipment

It's good to have several bowls of varying sizes, a couple of wooden spoons, a flexible spatula and a set of decent cake tins.

Electric Tools

I find a hand-held electric beater makes short work of whisking the butter with the sugar and adding the eggs. Free-standing mixers are excellent, too, but can take up space in a small kitchen, and I have found it pointless to have equipment that is not kept out on the side ready for use. In my experience, anything put into a cupboard has a strange tendency to stay in the cupboard. Food processors can be used for cake- and biscuit-making, but it is very important not to over-process the mix. The speed of these machines means that you must watch carefully, or the mix will be over-worked. This is the time to learn to use the pulse button.

Cake Pans, Tins and Sheets

Cake pans and baking sheets should be of good quality. You don't need a huge collection of pans, but the ones you do have should be in good condition. Cheap tinned metal pans soon lose their protective surface and can rust. Whilst not harmful, this rust will taint the flavour of your cakes and biscuits. I like to use heavy anodized aluminium cake pans which, while costly, will last a lifetime.

I would suggest you need three round sandwich tins, two loaf tins of varying sizes, two bun trays, three baking sheets and a springform tin. You can naturally accessorize your baking drawer with tins of many shapes and sizes and now colours. I have recently bought a couple of flexible silicone pans, one octagonal and one heart-shaped. Add in a madeleine pan and a savarin mould, and you will soon be able to set up as a commercial baker!

Liners for Tins

I line my tins with Teflon or silicone sheets cut to size. A costlier option than greaseproof (waxed) paper or baking parchment at the start, but the delight of having cakes, breads and biscuits slip effortlessly out of the tin or off the tray makes the expense worthwhile. Both the silicone and Teflon sheets are readily available from cook shops and larger supermarkets. Cut to size and left in the tin they will last years. If you are still relying on greaseproof or parchment paper for lining, place your tin on the paper, and draw around the outside edges. Cut this out for the base. Measure the height of the sides, and cut an oblong piece of paper to fit. Grease the tin first, and then slot your paper in.

I also keep a selection of different-sized paper muffin and bun cases (cups), plus some disposable icing bags.

Storing Cakes and Biscuits

Store cakes and biscuits in airtight tins. Whilst I do have a wonderful range of old biscuit and toffee tins from years back, I prefer now to use hard plastic boxes with clip-on lids for the oh-so-simple reason that you can see what is in each container and don't have those moments of discovery when opening a tin of mouldy cake that has got lost at the back of the pantry.

Some cakes keep better than others, and indeed some really improve with keeping. All dense fruit cakes will mature nicely for a couple of months. I have kept my Baton Rouge cake for over six months, and my easy gingerbread gets stickier as the days pass.

If you're making filled biscuits, make and store the unfilled cookies, adding the filling just before you want to serve them.

Remember also that biscuits, whether sweet or savoury, if they have been in the tin for a while, can be refreshed by popping them into a 180ºC/350ºF/Gas Mark 4 oven for 5–10 minutes.

❧❧❧

Home baking is a delight, and so much easier than it might seem. It fills your house with wonderful aromas and your family with wonderful treats. So get to it.

Classic Sponge Cake

A classic sponge recipe is part of any cook's repertoire. Once you have mastered it, you can adapt it to fit a myriad of purposes. It makes simple layer cakes, iced loaf cakes, or the mixture can be divided to make twelve buns (cook for 15–17 minutes). You can mix in chopped cherries, raisins, use lemon juice or almond essence instead of vanilla... These small pointers will help you achieve success every time.

❖ The soft butter should be beaten with the caster (superfine) sugar until the mixture is pale and light. This is called 'creaming', though I can't fathom why when no cream is used. The sugar should begin to dissolve and the mixture become less gritty.

❖ Next, it's important that the eggs are at room temperature before you start. This will allow the egg to form a good emulsion with the butter/sugar mixture, which means that the mixture won't curdle.

❖ The flour should be lightly folded in once the eggs have been added. Don't over-work the mixture at this stage as you don't want to overly expand the gluten, which will make the cake tough.

❖ Have the oven well preheated so that once the cake is in the tins it can be baked immediately, so getting the best result from the baking powder which is the rising agent.

❖ The proportions for a classic sponge are simple: the weight of eggs in fat, flour and sugar.

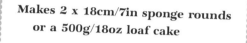

Makes 2 x 18cm/7in sponge rounds or a 500g/18oz loaf cake

1 teaspoon baking powder
120g/4½oz/scant 1¼ cups plain
    (all-purpose) flour
120g/4½oz/½ cup soft butter, plus a little
    extra for greasing
125g/4¼oz/scant ¾ cup caster
    (superfine) sugar
1 teaspoon vanilla extract
2 large eggs (these will weigh approx.
    60g/2½oz each)

Preheat the oven to 180ºC/350ºF/Gas Mark 4, and grease a couple of 18cm/7in round sponge tins with extra butter, and base-line with greaseproof (waxed) paper. You could also use a single 500g/18oz loaf tin.

Sift the baking powder with the flour and set aside.

In a large bowl, beat the butter, sugar and vanilla together until the mixture is light and fluffy.

Beat the eggs together in a small bowl. Now add the egg mixture a little at a time to the butter mixture, beating well between each addition. If the mixture splits (curdles), add a spoonful of flour with each helping of egg.

Once all the egg is in, fold in the flour using a metal spoon, then put the mixture into your prepared tins.

Bake in the preheated oven for 20–25 minutes. (The loaf cake will take a little longer, about 30–35 minutes.) You can tell the cake is cooked, as the sponge will be well risen and golden brown and it will be pulling gently from the side of the tin.

Cool on a wire rack for 5 minutes before removing from the tin and leaving to cool completely.

Sandwich layer cakes together with jam or butter cream; I love whipped cream and sliced strawberries. The layer cake can be iced with glacé icing or topped with cherries before baking.

Baton Rouge Cake

Makes 1 large cake (cuts into 14 slices)

225g/8oz/1¼ cups whole glacé
(candied) cherries
225g/8oz/1¼ cups candied pineapple
chunks
225g/8oz/1¼ cups pecan halves
350g/12oz/2¼ cups stoned dates
200g/7oz/1 cup light muscovado sugar
3 large eggs, beaten
140g/5oz/1¼ cups plain (all-purpose)
flour
1 teaspoon baking powder
½ teaspoon fine sea salt
125ml/4fl oz/½ cup brandy or
American bourbon,
plus extra for 'feeding'

Topping
200g/7oz/¾ cup apricot jam
225g/8oz/1½ cups ready-to-eat apricots
125g/4½oz/1 cup pecan nut halves

This wonderful fruit cake comes from America, New Orleans in fact, where they particularly like bourbon-laced desserts. It keeps wonderfully well. I had one in my larder, well wrapped in waxed paper and foil, for over a year. I added a drop or two more of bourbon and it was delicious. I usually make one of these a couple of months before Christmas, lacing it often, ready for the big day.

Keep the pieces of fruit quite large in this wonderful cake, so that they look good when the cake is sliced. I prefer not to ice the cake but glaze with apricot jam and arrange more dried fruit and nuts on the top.

Preheat the oven to 160°C/320°F/Gas Mark 3, and line a 20cm/8in cake tin with non-stick paper.

Mix all the ingredients for the cake together well (the mix will look a little odd, but don't worry). Turn the mixture into the lined tin, and bake in the preheated oven for 60–70 minutes, or until the cake just begins to pull from the sides of the tin. Test for doneness by inserting a thin metal skewer into the middle of the cake. If it comes out clean, the cake is ready.

Cool on a rack before wrapping closely in greaseproof (waxed) paper. Once a week for four weeks, unwrap the cake and spoon over an extra couple of tablespoons of brandy.

To top the cake, warm the jam in a saucepan, adding about 2 tablespoons of water to thin, if necessary. Now rub the warmed jam through a sieve to remove any lumps. Paint a thin layer of jam glaze on top of the cake. Arrange the apricots and pecans on the cake, then brush over generously with the jam glaze. This cake keeps for months if well wrapped in wax paper and stored in an airtight tin.

Christmas Pudding

Serves 8–10

500g/18oz/3⅓ cups mixed dried fruit (raisins, currants, sultanas/golden raisins)

115g/4oz/⅝ cup pitted ready-to-eat prunes, chopped

115g/4oz/½ cup dark muscovado sugar

4 tablespoons dark rum

150ml/5fl oz/scant ¾ cup stout (I use Murphy's)

115g/4oz/scant ¾ cup frozen butter, grated

55g/2oz/½ cup plain (all-purpose) flour

115g/4oz/scant 2 cups fresh breadcrumbs

115g/4oz/1⅓ cups ground almonds

115g/4oz/1 cup walnut halves, chopped

115g/4oz/1 cup blanched almonds, chopped

½ teaspoon freshly grated nutmeg

1 teaspoon ground cinnamon

2 teaspoons mixed spice

115g/4oz/¾ cup glacé (candied) cherries, chopped (the bright unfashionable red ones are best, as they look more festive)

3 eggs, beaten

There is a simple secret to making a good Christmas pudding: use only the best fruit and freshest nuts and spices, and steam it for as long as you can bear to! It really makes a huge difference to the colour and taste of the pudding if you can steam for 8 or so hours. Don't panic, this does not need to be done in one day. I often steam my puddings over two or three days, and have never had any problems with them.

Sixpences should be wrapped in foil. I'm sure there are health and safety reasons why we should not put charms or money in the pudding, but Christmas is a H & S nightmare anyway, with charms being the least of one's problems...

Put the mixed dried fruit, prunes, sugar, rum and stout into a bowl and leave for 24 hours.

In a large bowl, toss the grated butter with the flour and breadcrumbs. Add the ground almonds, the chopped nuts, spices and cherries. Now add the fruit mixture and the beaten eggs. Mix well, let the family have a stir and a wish, cover the bowl with a cloth and then leave in a cool place overnight.

Press the mixture into one 900ml/2 pint or two 600ml/1 pint pudding basins. Cover with two rounds of greaseproof (waxed) paper and then with foil and secure with string. Leave space for expansion, as with steak and kidney pudding (see page 80).

Steam the large pudding for 8–10 hours, the smaller ones for 4–6 hours. You can use a steamer, or a large saucepan with an upturned saucer or trivet in it, and enough water to come halfway up the sides of the pudding bowl (see also page 80).

Spotted Dick

Serves 6

115g/4oz/1¾ cups suet, fresh (see
    page 158) or packet
115g/4oz/1 cup self-raising flour
60g/2¼oz/¾ cup ground almonds
60g/2¼oz/1 cup stale cake or white
    breadcrumbs
85g/3oz/½ cup raisins, dried cranberries
    or dried sour cherries
3 tablespoons soft brown sugar
1 egg, beaten
a squeeze of lemon juice
about 150ml/5fl oz/⅓ cup milk, to mix

For the bowl
butter
2–3 tablespoons golden syrup

Every child has laughed at the name of this pudding, but most love it. I know the child in me does.

Using fresh suet lifts the flavour to a whole new level, and replacing half of the flour with cake or breadcrumbs makes it very light.

Combine all the ingredients for the pudding in a large bowl, mixing to a firm but moist consistency.

Butter a 1 litre/1¾ pint pudding basin generously, then pour in the golden syrup. Pile the pudding mixture on top. Cover with two rounds of greaseproof (waxed) paper and then with foil and secure with string. Leave space for expansion, as with steak and kidney pudding (see page 80).

Steam the pudding for 2 hours in a steamer or saucepan half filled with hot water (as described in the steak and kidney pudding on page 80). Make sure the water is kept at a simmer and don't let the saucepan boil dry.

Unwrap the pudding and then turn carefully out of the bowl on to a dish.

Cut into wedges, and eat with cream.

A real, old fashioned custard would be perfect with this pudding, but if you want to pretend you're counting calories some crème fraîche would be good.

Every pantry should have a tin of flapjack ready and waiting for all those hungry moments. This is my favourite version, a simple syrupy oat bar. Sometimes, when the mood takes me, I toss in some raisins or coconut to give added texture and a rather different flavour.

Preheat the oven to 180°C/350°F/Gas Mark 4, and have ready an 18cm/7in square baking tin.

In a medium saucepan melt the syrup, butter and sugar together over a low heat. Stir until the sugar has almost dissolved – it may not quite disappear into the buttery mass. The important thing here is not to let the mixture boil.

Now stir in the oats. At first there will seem to be too many to mix in, but keep going and soon you will have a sticky mass. Spread this into the baking tin and bake in the preheated oven for 25–30 minutes, or until an evenly coloured, golden brown.

Allow to cool in the tin before cutting into squares and storing in an airtight container. The flapjacks will keep for three to four weeks.

Flapjack

Makes 12–18 bars

2 tablespoons golden syrup
225g/8oz/2 sticks butter, cut into pieces
175g/6oz/¾ cup soft or unrefined brown
  sugar
225g/8oz/2¾ cups coarse or rolled
  porridge oats

Fruit & Nut Carrot Cake

Serves 8–10

175g/6oz/1¾ cups plain (all-purpose) flour,
  plus extra for dusting
butter, for greasing
1 teaspoon baking powder
1 teaspoon bicarbonate of soda (baking
  soda)
¼ teaspoon fine sea salt
3 teaspoons mixed spice
175ml/6fl oz/¾ cup sunflower oil
3 eggs, beaten
175g/6oz/¾ cup soft brown sugar
60g/2¼oz/½ cup ready-to-eat prunes,
  chopped
60g/2¼oz/½ cup walnut halves, roughly
  chopped
175g/6oz/1⅓ cups carrots, peeled weight,
  finely grated

Frosting
55g/2oz/¼ cup cream cheese
115g/4oz/½ cup icing (confectioners') sugar
½ teaspoon finely grated lemon rind

A simple cake to make and one that improves with keeping. I store it in an airtight tin, wrapped in clingfilm (plastic wrap) or waxed paper, for up to two weeks. It's best to ice the cake on the day you need it, as cream cheese frosting doesn't keep well. If you prefer, a simple lemon drizzle icing works well.

Preheat the oven to 180°C/350°F/Gas Mark 4, and have ready a greased and floured 900g/2lb loaf tin.

Sift the flour, baking powder, soda, salt and spice into a large bowl, making sure they are well mixed.

Whisk or blend together the oil, eggs and brown sugar until smooth. Stir this mixture, with the prunes, walnuts and carrots, into the flour. Fold everything together well and pour into the loaf tin.

Bake in the preheated oven for 50–60 minutes or until a skewer inserted in the centre comes out clean.

Allow to cool for 5 minutes before turning out on to a rack until completely cold. Either wrap and store in an airtight tin or ice and serve.

To make the frosting, beat everything together until smooth. Spread the frosting over the top of the loaf cake and allow it to set for about an hour. Serve cut into thick slices.

Golden Gingerbread

Serves 20

175g/6oz/1½ sticks butter
225g/8oz/scant 1¼ cups soft brown sugar
350g/12oz/1 cup golden syrup
1 egg
300ml/10fl oz/1¼ cups milk
450g/1lb/4½ cups self-raising flour
½ teaspoon fine sea salt
1½ teaspoons ground ginger

This is exactly the sort of cake you might hope to find in granny's larder. Sticky and moist, it keeps on improving as the days pass (but is best eaten within three weeks). I love the last few slices spread with butter.

For a darker cake, substitute some of the syrup with treacle.

Preheat the oven to 180ºC/350ºF/Gas Mark 4, and paper-line or grease a large shallow tin of about 33 x 22 x 5cm/13 x 8½ x 2in.

Put the butter, sugar and syrup into a saucepan and heat very gently for about 10 minutes until everything melts. Cool a little and then beat in the egg and the milk. Mix in the dry ingredients and pour into the prepared tin.

Bake in the preheated oven for 70–85 minutes or until well risen and firm to the touch.

Allow to cool in the tin, then cut into squares and store in an airtight container for 48 hours before eating.

Panforte di Siena

Serves 20

350g/12oz/2 cups whole unskinned
    almonds
60g/2¼oz/½ cup walnut halves
1 cinnamon stick
1 tablespoon coriander seeds
6 cloves
6 black peppercorns
1 teaspoon freshly grated nutmeg
1 heaped tablespoon cocoa powder
250g/9oz/1⅓ cups caster (superfine) sugar
115g/4oz/⅓ cup clear honey
450g/1lb/3½ cups whole preserved
    candied fruit, chopped
35g/1¼oz/⅓ cup plain (all-purpose) flour,
    sifted

To bake and finish
rice paper (available from specialist
    cake shops)
1 tablespoon icing (confectioners') sugar
1 tablespoon cornflour (cornstarch)

Preheat the oven to 180°C/350°F/Gas Mark 4, and line the base of a 20cm/8in springform cake tin with rice paper.

Roast the almonds and walnuts in the preheated oven until golden, about 8–10 minutes. Either grind all the spices plus the walnuts in a coffee grinder, or pound the cinnamon stick, walnuts, coriander seeds, cloves and peppercorns in a pestle and mortar. Stir in the nutmeg and cocoa powder.

Heat the caster (superfine) sugar and honey in a small saucepan, stirring continuously until the mixture comes to a gentle rolling boil. Continue to stir for half a minute, then remove from the heat. Stir in the whole almonds, the candied fruit, the walnut and cocoa mixture and sifted flour.

Pack the mixture into the lined cake tin. It is very hot and stiff at this stage, so work as quickly as you can, flattening it down into the tin with the back of a spoon. Cut more rice paper to fit and cover the top of the *panforte*.

Bake in the preheated oven for 30 minutes. Remove from the oven and leave to cool slightly, in the tin, for a few minutes. You need to remove it from the tin whilst it is still warm, so don't leave it for too long. Run a palette knife around the edge of the tin to loosen the sides, and press up from the base. Lift the *panforte* from the base and, using your hands, press any loose bits back into shape.

Once completely cold, dust with a mixture of icing (confectioners') sugar and cornflour (cornstarch).

Panforte keeps for months wrapped in greaseproof (waxed) paper and stored in an airtight tin.

Panforte – *'strong bread' in Italian – dates from the fourteenth century, when the spice trade was starting to flourish in Italy. Traditionally made in December, it symbolized a prosperous New Year. Serve cut into small pieces – it is very sweet! – as a sweetmeat in place of or after desserts, with coffee or a glass of sweet wine.*

Chocolate Biscuit Cake

Serves 10

200g/7oz digestive biscuits
85g/3oz/½ cup blanched slivered almonds
85g/3oz/½ cup glacé (candied) cherries, halved
1 egg, beaten
2 tablespoons caster (superfine) sugar
2 tablespoons Grand Marnier liqueur (optional)
200g/7oz/1¾ sticks butter, cut into pieces
200g/7oz plain chocolate, broken into pieces

Much too delicious to last long, this simple no-bake chocolate cake can be made with a variety of plain biscuits. I favour rich tea or digestive. I use plain chocolate in the mixture, but a wonderful dark chocolate scented with spice or orange would be just fine, too.

Break the biscuits into 1cm/½in pieces and place in a bowl. Add the nuts and cherries. Beat the egg with the caster (superfine) sugar and liqueur (if using) until the sugar has completely dissolved. Pour this over the biscuit mixture, then toss everything together.

Melt the butter and chocolate over a low heat in a small pan, stirring well. (If you prefer, you can melt the butter with the chocolate in a microwave at a low heat, 450, for 5 minutes, checking after 3 minutes.) Pour the hot chocolate over the biscuit mixture and mix thoroughly.

Spoon the cake into a 900g/2lb loaf tin, level the top and place in the fridge for about 3 hours to set.

To unmould, dip the tin into hot water for about 15 seconds, then turn out on to a plate. Cut into thin slices to serve.

Keep in the fridge for a week, and please remember that this cake contains raw egg.

Basic Baking Mix

Makes approx. 600g/1lb 5oz

500g/18oz/4½ cups plain (all-purpose)
   flour
2 tablespoons baking powder
1½ teaspoons fine sea salt
115g/4oz vegetable shortening

*This is a wonderful mix to have handy
and is much used in North America where
it can be bought commercially. My recipe
comes from a friend, who tells me she had
it from her mother's cook! Essentially, it is
flour ready rubbed with fat. You must use
the white vegetable shortening found in
most supermarket chiller cabinets. The
joy of the mix is that you can use it as
the basis for many scones, rock cakes
or waffles, adding your own flavourings.*

Sift together the flour, baking powder
and salt. When well combined, cut in the
shortening using the paddle attachment
of the mixer.

Store in the fridge or a cold larder for
up to one month.

Scones

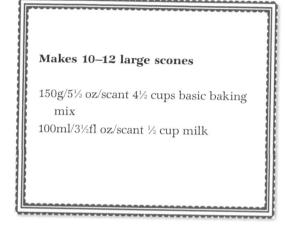

Makes 10–12 large scones

150g/5½ oz/scant 4½ cups basic baking
  mix
100ml/3½fl oz/scant ½ cup milk

This is one way of using the basic baking mix, opposite.

Preheat the oven to 200ºC/400ºF/Gas Mark 6.

Put the basic baking mix into a bowl and stir in the milk, using a fork. For richer scones, use buttermilk or natural yoghurt.

Turn out onto a lightly floured board and knead for about 30 seconds, being careful not to over-work the dough. Roll into a circle 1cm/½in thick. Cut into scones using a floured biscuit cutter or slice into wedges. Place on a baking sheet. Press the centres of the biscuits with your thumb or the back of a spoon, and brush lightly with extra cream or milk.

Bake in the preheated oven for 10–15 minutes. Eat warm, split and filled with butter, jam and clotted or whipped cream.

Waffles & Pancakes

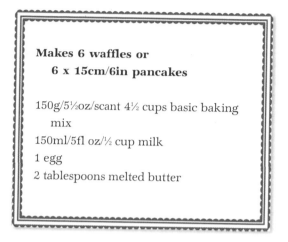

**Makes 6 waffles or
  6 x 15cm/6in pancakes**

150g/5½oz/scant 4½ cups basic baking
  mix
150ml/5fl oz/½ cup milk
1 egg
2 tablespoons melted butter

Yet another way... This recipe also makes excellent American-style pancakes if you don't have a waffle iron. Add chopped pecans, or fresh blueberries.

Whisk everything together lightly. Don't worry about lumps, they will disappear as the waffles cook.

To make waffles, heat the waffle iron until hot and then add about 4 tablespoons of mix. Close the lid and cook until steam stops coming from the iron.

Serve with maple syrup, melted butter and crisp bacon.

To cook pancakes, warm a dry frying pan over a moderate heat until hot (about 5 minutes). Pour 1 tablespoon of vegetable oil into the pan and swirl it about. Spoon in the mixture, about a large tablespoon at a time. Now, if you want, you can dot on some blueberries or scatter over some chopped nuts.

Wait until small bubbles begin to break, then turn the pancakes over and cook the other side for about 60 seconds. Serve at once, with bacon and maple syrup.

Almond Petticoat Tail Shortbread

Makes 1 x 20cm/8in biscuit

140g/5oz/1¼ cups plain (all-purpose) flour
55g/2oz/scant ¾ cup freshly ground almonds
115g/4oz/1 stick cold butter, plus extra for greasing
55g/2oz/½ cup caster (superfine) sugar

To finish
8 blanched whole almonds
extra caster (superfine) sugar

Rich buttery shortbread is one of life's treats. Whilst a petticoat tail is a traditional shape for shortbread, I often make fingers or squares by pressing the mixture into the appropriate shaped tin.

In this recipe I've added ground almonds but these are not strictly necessary; you can replace them with a further 55g/2oz/4½ cups plain (all-purpose) flour.

In a large bowl mix the flour and almonds. Cut the butter into small pieces and rub it into the flour until the mixture resembles breadcrumbs. Add the sugar and work the mixture with your hands until it forms a dough. Work quickly as you don't want the mixture to get too warm and the butter oily. Roll into a ball, wrap in clingfilm (plastic wrap), and chill for 30 minutes.

Preheat the oven to 190°C/375°F/Gas Mark 5.

Gently roll out the ball of dough to give a circle about 20cm/8in in diameter. Place on a lightly greased baking sheet and, using a sharp knife, mark the circle into eight. Don't cut through the dough, just mark the surface. Prick the circle all over with a sharp fork, then press an almond into the outer edge of each marked petticoat tail. Sprinkle generously with caster (superfine) sugar and bake in the preheated oven for 25 minutes or until very lightly browned.

Remove from the oven and leave to cool on a rack. This shortbread keeps well, for up to six weeks, if wrapped in waxed paper or clingfilm and stored in an airtight tin. It can also be frozen.

Having a tin of brandy snaps in the pantry gives you a start when serving simple desserts like ice-cream or summer fruits – allowing you a really professional touch when you pipe in flavoured cream just before serving.

You can make the brandy snaps any size and either roll them, drape them over a bottle or rolling pin, or even mould hot brandy snaps over a ramekin dish to make edible baskets in which to serve ice-cream. Only cook about four at a time as the biscuits cool quickly once you remove them from the oven and they will break as you shape them.

Heat the oven to 180°C/350°F/Gas Mark 4, and grease a couple of baking sheets with extra butter.

Put the flour into a bowl and into the oven for 3–4 minutes to warm. Melt the sugar, butter and syrup together in a medium pan. Mix in the warmed flour, ginger, lemon juice and brandy.

Drop spoonfuls of the mixture, well spaced, on to the greased baking sheets and bake in the preheated oven until brown, about 4–6 minutes. Watch carefully, as they overcook easily.

Remove the trays from the oven, cool for a few moments, and then lift the biscuits with a palette knife and quickly shape (see above). If you want to roll the brandy snaps in the traditional way, only cook a few at a time. Repeat until all the mixture is used. Once cooled, store the brandy snaps in an airtight tin for up to four weeks.

Brandy Snaps

Makes 15–20

115g/4oz/1 cup plain (all-purpose) flour
115g/4oz/¾ cup granulated sugar
115g/4oz/1 stick butter, broken into pieces, plus extra for greasing
115g/4oz/⅓ cup golden syrup
1 teaspoon ground ginger
juice of ½ lemon
1 tablespoon brandy

Whip double (heavy) cream until stiff and flavour with almond essence, orange liqueur, brandy, or whatever you like, then pipe into the snaps. Fill them just before serving, not more than 30 minutes before, or they will soften.

Cantuccini

Makes approx. 24 biscuits

250g/9oz/2¼ cups plain (all-purpose) flour
250g/9oz/1¼ cups caster (superfine) sugar
½ teaspoon baking powder
fine sea salt
½ teaspoon vanilla extract
1 egg, at room temperature
2 whole eggs, plus 1 egg yolk
100g/3½oz/½ cup each of almonds and
     pistachio nuts, roughly chopped
1 teaspoon whole aniseeds, crushed
1 egg white, to glaze

*These twice-baked biscuits are a perfect
addition to anyone's store-cupboard.
They are simplicity to make, but you must
remember one point: whilst the mix will
seem ridiculously dry at the beginning
during the kneading, you must have faith
and keep going. It will come together and
form a dough!*

*Using dried cranberries as well as
nuts makes these biscuits more festive.
Substitute dried cranberries for the
almonds. If you can't find aniseed,
use vanilla seeds.*

Preheat the oven to 180ºC/350ºF/Gas Mark 4, and have ready a baking tray lined with non-stick paper.

Put the flour, sugar, baking powder, a pinch of salt, the vanilla, eggs and egg yolk into a bowl and mix until the dough becomes sticky. Add the nuts (or nuts and cranberries) and aniseed, and mix until well combined. There will seem to be too many nuts, but keep going.

Divide the paste in two. Roll each piece out into log shapes, about 3cm/1¼in wide. Put on the lined baking tray. Keep the logs at least 5cm/2in apart, as they spread while cooking. Brush with beaten egg white and bake in the preheated oven for 30–35 minutes, or until pale gold but not soft.

Remove the baking tray from the oven and reduce the temperature to 150ºC/300ºF/Gas Mark 2. Cut each of the logs diagonally into twelve slices and return these slices to the baking sheet. Return the biscuits to the oven and allow to bake at this gentle heat until crisp, about another 30–45 minutes.

Allow to cool and store in an airtight tin for up to six months. Serve with a sweet wine like Vin Santo, or little cups of espresso.

Lemon Crunch Creams

Makes approx. 12 biscuits

115g/4oz/1 stick soft butter, cut into
    pieces, plus extra for greasing
115g/4oz/½ cup caster (superfine) sugar
finely grated zest and juice of 1 large
    lemon
1 tablespoon cornflour (cornstarch)
140g/5oz/1¼ cups plain (all-purpose) flour

Butter icing
55g/2oz/½ stick butter, softened
175g/6oz/¾ cup icing (confectioners')
    sugar
a squeeze of lemon juice

*Home-made custard creams? Yes, and they
are so simple to make – almost as easy as
they are to eat. Once filled with the cream
filling the biscuits will soften, so fill just
before serving.*

Preheat the oven to 180ºC/350ºF/Gas Mark 4,
and grease a baking sheet with extra
butter. Have ready a piping (decorating) bag
fitted with a star nozzle.

In a large bowl, and using a wooden
spoon, cream the butter with the sugar
then beat in the lemon zest and juice. Mix
together until the mixture is smooth and
creamy. Sift on the cornflour (cornstarch)
and plain (all-purpose) flour and mix these
in well.

Fill the piping bag with the dough,
and pipe small biscuits about 5cm/2in long
on to the prepared baking sheet. Bake
the biscuits in the preheated oven for
12–15 minutes or until the edges are
touched with a light golden brown. Cool
on a wire rack, and store in an airtight tin
if not filling immediately. The biscuits will
last unfilled for up to four weeks.

To finish the biscuits, make the
butter icing. Beat the butter and icing
(confectioners') sugar together, adding
lemon juice to taste. Use this to sandwich
two biscuits together.

Whip a little peanut butter into the buttercream or try some melted chocolate to vary the flavours.

These light biscuits are ideal for serving with fruit fools. They are the classic trifle sponge, and essential for lining the tin when making rich cream Charlottes.

Preheat the oven to 200°C/400°F/Gas Mark 6, and grease a couple of baking sheets with some butter. Have ready a large piping (decorating) bag fitted with a plain nozzle.

Place the sugar and egg yolks in a large bowl. Using an electric mixer, whisk the mixture until you have a dense foam. Beat in the vanilla and zest.

Sift the flour and salt over the foam and then, using a metal spoon, cut and fold the flour into the egg.

Spoon the mixture into the piping bag and pipe 10cm/4in long thin biscuits on to the prepared baking sheets. Bake in the preheated oven for 7–10 minutes, or until a light golden brown.

Remove from the tray while still warm and cool on a wire rack. Store in an air-tight tin until needed, for up to one month.

Sponge Finger Biscuits

Makes approx. 20 biscuits

butter, for greasing
100g/3½oz/½ cup caster (superfine) sugar
3 egg yolks
½ teaspoon vanilla extract
a little finely grated lemon or orange zest
100g/3½oz/scant 1 cup plain (all-purpose) flour
a pinch of fine sea salt

Blue Cheese & Sesame Biscuits

Makes approx. 20 biscuits

115g/4oz/1 cup self-raising flour
  (or plain/all-purpose flour with
  1 teaspoon baking powder),
  gluten-free flour is best
85g/3oz/¾ stick butter, plus extra
  for greasing
85g/3oz Dolcelatte or other creamy
  blue cheese
approx. 3 tablespoons grated Parmesan
  cheese
2–3 tablespoons sesame seeds

What I particularly love about these delicious crumbly biscuits is that they are best made with gluten-free flour, so they are perfect for those who can't digest wheat. They can be made with almost any cheese you have in the larder. Just keep the proportions the same, and don't cut back on the butter.

The biscuits can be made in moments, and keep well in an airtight tin. If you have time, warm them through in the oven before serving.

Place all the ingredients apart from the sesame seeds in the bowl of a food processor and whiz, using short bursts of power, until you have a dough. Alternatively, use your fingers to rub the butter into the flour, then add the crumbled blue cheese and the Parmesan. Make sure it is thoroughly mixed together. Wrap the dough in clingfilm (plastic wrap), and chill for 1 hour.

Meanwhile, preheat the oven to 220°C/425°F/Gas Mark 7, and grease a baking sheet with extra butter.

Take the dough out of the fridge, and take off small pieces about the size of cherries. Roll these into balls, then roll in the sesame seeds. Place on the greased baking sheet, and make an indentation in the centre of each one with your thumb.

Bake in the preheated oven for 7–10 minutes. The biscuits are ready when a mid-golden brown. Cool on a rack before serving, with dry sherry or other aperitifs.

Thyme-scented Oatcakes

Makes 18–20

115g/4oz/scant 1½ cups fine oatmeal
¼ teaspoon fine sea salt
½ teaspoon chopped fresh thyme leaves
1 tablespoon olive oil
4–5 tablespoons boiling water

Home-made biscuits for cheese – how good is that? These are delicious with Cheddar or Stilton, but also with peanut butter and jam.

Preheat the oven to 160ºC/320ºF/Gas Mark 3.
Pour the oatmeal, salt, thyme and oil into a food processor and mix for 60 seconds. Add the boiling water and continue to process for a further 90 seconds.
Turn the paste out on to a floured board and knead lightly. While the dough is warm, roll it out 2mm/¹⁄₁₆in thick and cut into 5cm/2in rounds or triangles. Place on a greased baking sheet.
Bake in the preheated oven for 15 minutes until crisp but only lightly coloured. Cool on a rack, and then store, for up to six weeks, in an airtight tin.

These are savoury oatcakes but can be sweetened by the addition of a teaspoon of sugar. You could even add some dried fruit, say 30g/1oz dried cranberries, to the mixture in the food processor, whizzing until finely chopped.

Cheddar & Celery Wafers

Makes approx. 48 wafers

175g/6oz/1½ cups plain (all-purpose) flour
85g/3oz/¾ stick cold butter, cut into
    pieces, plus extra for greasing
115g/4oz/scant 1 cup mature (sharp)
    Cheddar cheese, grated
1 teaspoon celery salt
1 egg yolk
1 teaspoon Dijon mustard
cold water, to mix

These crisp biscuits are delicious with sherry or, even better, a Bloody Mary.

Put the flour in a large bowl, and rub the butter into it until the mixture resembles fine breadcrumbs. Stir in the cheese and celery salt.

Beat the egg with the mustard and 3 tablespoons of cold water. Add this to the crumbs and mix to make a firm dough, adding extra water if needed. Form the dough into a ball, wrap in clingfilm (plastic wrap), and chill for 30 minutes.

Preheat the oven to 190ºC/375ºF/Gas Mark 5, and grease some baking sheets with extra butter.

Unwrap the dough and roll it out very thinly. Cut into biscuits using a 4cm/1½in round cutter. Place on the greased baking sheet and bake in the preheated oven for 8–12 minutes or until the biscuits are lightly golden all over. Remove from the oven and cool on a rack.

Store in an airtight tin, for up to four weeks.

Meringue Kisses

Makes 20–30

butter, for greasing
4 egg whites
225g/8oz/1¼ cups caster (superfine) sugar

Optional additions (use 1 only)
25g/1oz/scant 1¼ cups dark chocolate,
    grated
25g/1oz/scant ¼ cup dried cherries,
    finely chopped
55g/2oz/¾ cup desiccated
    (dry, unsweetened) coconut

The thing about meringues is that everyone loves them, and can always find room for a couple more. They are the perfect store-cupboard standby as they keep well – I've kept them for a couple of months – and can be served with whatever is to hand. Some ice-cream, fresh cream, yoghurt, tinned fruit and/or a splash of liqueur, and you have your pudding.

I vary the basic recipe, adding grated chocolate, chopped dried cherries or coconut, but only once the egg-white mixture is stiff and ready. With these lumpy ingredients you might need to choose a larger nozzle if piping the kisses, or you could just dollop out small spoonfuls on to your baking sheet.

Preheat the oven to 140ºC/280ºF/Gas Mark 1, and grease a couple of baking sheets with a little butter.

Whisk the egg whites in a spotlessly clean bowl until stiff. Gradually whisk in the sugar. Once you have added it all, keep on whisking until the mixture is very stiff and glossy.

Using a clean spoon, stir in the chocolate, chopped dried cherries or dessicated coconut if desired.

Spoon the mixture into a piping bag fitted with a star nozzle and pipe small meringues, about 3cm/1inch wide, on to the prepared baking sheets. Bake in the preheated oven for 30–40 minutes. The meringues will be crisp and pale cream in colour.

Allow to cool for a few moments before removing to a wire rack, using a fish slice/palette knife. Allow to cool completely. Once cold, store in an airtight tin for up to two months.

Salted caramel is now very fashionable, but I have always loved a sweet/salt combination, going so far as to mixing my popcorn at the cinema half and half.

I used a packet of roast salted peanuts for this recipe, but any plain roasted, salted nuts would be fine. Just avoid the highly flavoured dry-roast variety.

Line a 20cm/8in square tin with non-stick silicone or Teflon paper.

Place the sugar in a large shallow frying pan and put this over a medium heat. Cook until the sugar begins to melt, swirling the pan from time to time. You need to watch carefully so as not to over-brown the caramel. If you stir the sugar it will crystallize but sometimes this is inevitable. If the caramel looks grainy add the water, very carefully, and stir until the sugar is smooth. This should take about 8 minutes.

Once you have a smooth dark caramel, tip in the nuts, stir quickly and then pour into the prepared dish.

Allow the brittle to cool and set, then tap with a heavy knife to break it up into manageable pieces. Store, wrapped in waxed paper, in an airtight tin. It will keep for at least six weeks if you hide it on a high shelf...

Salted Peanut Brittle

Makes 650g/1lb 7oz

500g/18oz/scant 2¾ cups white sugar
2 tablespoons water
200g/7oz/scant 1¼ cups salted nuts

Nutty Vanilla & Maple Granola

Makes approx. 1kg/2¼lb

400g/14oz/5 cups rolled oats
100g/3½oz/1⅓ cups desiccated (dry, unsweetened) coconut
150g/5½oz/scant 2 cups coarse oatmeal
100g/3½oz/½ cup each of shelled pecan nuts and almonds
60g/2¼oz/⅓ cup sunflower seeds
150ml/5fl oz/½ cup vegetable oil
150g/5½oz/½ cup clear honey
100ml/3½fl oz/½ cup maple syrup
½–1 teaspoon fine sea salt
seeds from 1 vanilla pod

Making your own granola and muesli is very simple, and has the distinct advantage of you being in charge of the ingredients. If you hate coconut, for instance, just omit it. If, on the other hand, you are simply wild about macadamia nuts, use some of those. It's rather worrying to see just how much oil and sugar goes into granola; I have tried this recipe with less honey and less oil but it really isn't as good.

Preheat the oven to 180ºC/350ºF/Gas Mark 4, and line a baking sheet with silicone or other non-stick paper.

Mix the dry ingredients in a bowl. In a small pan, warm the oil, honey and maple syrup so they can be whisked together, then stir in the salt and vanilla seeds.

Pour this liquid mix over the dry mix and stir well to make sure everything is well coated. The mix will still be loose, but should look equally moist.

Spread the granola on to the lined baking sheet, and bake in the preheated oven for 30–45 minutes, stirring once or twice, until the mixture is a golden brown. (If you stir too often the granola will break up and not have enough chunks: I turn it over using a metal spatula to try and maintain the texture.) For a soft granola cook until lightly coloured; for a crunchy one, until a mid to dark gold.

Allow to cool before storing in an airtight container, for up to six weeks.

Making your own muesli is child's play, and indeed if you have children, it's one of the best ways to get them to eat a good breakfast. I like to use rolled organic oats because I like my breakfast to have a bit of chew, but for a softer muesli mix you could choose smaller porridge oats.

This mix makes a delicious porridge if cooked with milk or water in the usual fashion.

Mix everything together and store in an airtight container until needed.

You can serve the muesli dry with milk or fresh yoghurt (home-made is wonderful, see page 25), or you can serve it soaked. Several hours before you want to eat, the previous evening, say, measure a small coffee cup of muesli per person into a bowl and cover with apple juice. Leave to soak overnight and then serve with a dollop of yoghurt and a drizzle of runny honey.

This mixture can be eaten with milk, but is even better mixed with a couple of tablespoons of natural yogurt and half an apple, grated, and allowed to sit in a cold larder or fridge for 12–24 hours.

Seeded Cranberry Muesli

Makes approx. 475g/17oz

250g/9oz/scant 1¼ cups rolled oats
55g/2oz/¾ cup flaked almonds
35g/1¼oz/scant ¼ cup sunflower seeds
35g/1¼oz/scant ¼ cup pumpkin seeds
55g/2oz/⅓ cup dried cranberries
55g/2oz/⅓ cup raisins
2 teaspoons sesame seeds
2 teaspoons linseeds

SALT
CURING

Introduction

Salt has long been man's best friend when it comes to preserving food. In the days before refrigeration, salting and drying foods, sometimes with the addition of smoke, were the most commonly used methods of ensuring there was meat to eat during the long winter months. Preserving part of the carcass of a freshly killed animal meant the meat was available for several weeks or months after the butchering had taken place. The knock-on effects of this were many. If you could preserve part of your harvest, whether meat or fish, you could hunt less often. You were assured of food and could spend your time on other pursuits, be they intellectual or physical.

Salt was not seen as public enemy number one in those days, when heavy manual labour meant a considerable loss of salt from one's body through sweat. As salt is necessary for healthy body function, it needs to be replaced. Eating raw meat can replace some of this salt, but cooked meats, vegetables and grains contain very little salt unless it is added during the cooking process. So, whilst the food might have seemed salty to today's palates, much of the salt did form a necessary part of our ancestors' diets.

Salt, at first gathered from saltpans next to the sea, was harvested as a high-end crop. Roman soldiers were paid in salt, which is the origin of the word 'salary'. Salt, or the lack of it, has led to riots, taxes and migration on a massive scale – quite extraordinary for something we now take completely for granted.

The early trade in salt cod, a food essential across Europe for the many fast days of the Catholic Church, and still a European staple, was instrumental in the discovery and colonization of Newfoundland. (Cod were said to be so plentiful there that you could virtually walk across the water on the backs of the giant fish.) Having been caught and salted, the fish were dried and shipped back across the Atlantic. I have given a recipe for home-salted cod on page 129, but this type of salting is very different. In the traditional method, the fish is salted for several days then dried until leather-like in texture. It needs long soaking to reconstitute it and, when cooked, has a strong and distinct flavour so is often served with boiled potatoes and a rich garlic mayonnaise. And this salt fish should not be confused with stockfish, which is air-dried rather than salted.

The Action of Salt on Food

Salt preserving works by osmosis. The water from the less concentrated solution (i.e. the naturally occurring juices in the foods) will flow through the semi-permeable membranes of the meat, fish or vegetables into the concentrated solution (i.e. the brine or raw salt), and so the foods will become dryer. This leaching of water from the foods being salted removes the medium that bacteria and fungi like to live in. The food also becomes highly salted and so, again, becomes a very inhospitable host for the bacteria.

Koshering of meat to make it fit for consumption by orthodox Jews is done by removing the blood from the freshly butchered carcass by the addition of coarse but very pure kosher salt.

Salting itself is not sufficient to completely cure food, and once sufficient time has been spent in the salt or brine, the food must be dried before it is stored. In hot countries, sun-drying was an obvious choice, and in Scandinavian and Arctic countries wind-drying was effective. In damp central Europe, artificial heat was needed to dry the foods, and so they were often hung in the family kitchen chimney where they would smoke as well as dry. This chimney would act as a larder for meat and red herring as they would be stored here until needed, presumably becoming smokier by the day. The smoke had the added benefit of being an antibacterial agent, so aiding preservation. And the smoke seems to have been a very palatable flavour, as today we still smoke food for the taste benefit alone.

Dry Salting and Brining

There are two main methods of salting: dry salting, and immersing the fish or meat in a concentrated brine. Both methods have their virtues.

Dry Salting

Dry salting is often used when the salted food will then be dried or smoked. Dry-cure bacon and hams are felt to be more flavourful than those brined, as no water is added to the mix. The finished ham is dryer and the bacon less flabby, so both are more concentrated in flavour. Ham must be well salted and it needs the addition of sodium nitrate, which is used as an antibacterial agent. Home salting whole hams should be undertaken with great care. The bone should be removed and the cavity stuffed with salt, as it is this centre part, deep in the leg, where the cure takes most time to reach, and where the rot will start if the leg is not sufficiently cured. There are few things sadder than having to throw away your whole beautiful ham when you realise that the smell coming from the meat is a sign of rot because the cure wasn't sufficiently effective. The second problem with home curing hams is that the end product tends to taste powerfully of salt. This is not intended to put you off, however, and if you have access to a pig's hindquarter and have a dry shed or outhouse in which to hang your ham after curing, there are many books and Internet sites that can advise you.

Oily fish, such as herring, anchovy, sprats and sardines, do not dry well – the oil easily becoming rancid – so they are best dry salted. Some 6,000 fisherwomen were recorded in 1930 as following the herrings on their yearly migration from Orkney down the east coast of Britain, living at the ports where the trawlers would land their catch and gutting the fresh fish before packing them into barrels layered up with salt. Along the Mediterranean, anchovy and sardines are to this day salted and canned, ready for sale in the many fish markets.

Brining

Brining or 'wet salting' is a simpler technique than dry salting to use at home. I often salt meat to add flavour and create such traditional dishes as salt belly pork and salt brisket of beef. Whilst butchers will often salt these cuts for you, at home you can add your own aromatics and choose just how long you want the cure to be.

A simple brine consists of 100g/3½oz/½ cup salt for each litre/1¾ pints/scant ¼ cup of water. The salt is dissolved in a portion of hot water before the bulk of the water is added cold. Brine should always be used cold, and the pot containing the soaking meat put into either a cold larder or the fridge while the brine works.

Brines vary in strength, and many have aromatics and sugar added. In some cases, black treacle or molasses is added to brines used for meats.

Salt as a Cooking and Flavouring Agent

In the home, salt is most often used as a flavouring. In some fish recipes, though, the action of the salt 'cooks' the fish, in a similar way to lemon or lime juice. By this I mean the texture of the fish is altered and resembles lightly cooked fish once the salt has worked. It is for this reason that you shouldn't season with salt far in advance of cooking meat or fish, as this will draw out moisture.

Foods that are salted are often used as a flavouring agent. The preserved lemons on page 138 can be chopped and added to any number of dishes from mashed potatoes to tagines. We all know how moreish salted nuts are, and my new flavour sensation is the nutty dipping salt from North Africa, *dukkah*, on page 141. Salted anchovies make a wonderful addition to gravy. Simple pop a couple in the roasting pan before you add the flour, stir over the heat for a few moments to dissolve them, then continue as usual. The savoury flavour they add to the gravy is quite wonderful and not at all fishy. Perhaps it's best not to mention it to your family before they taste it, though...

I write about the various different types of salt in the condiments chapter (see page 210).

Equipment

Very little specialized equipment is needed, but you must bear in mind salt's corrosive properties, so glass and china bowls are best for mixing the brine. I use a solid polyurethane box with a clip-on lid for brining meat. This works well and keeps any odours out of the fridge.

When storing salted lemons or other citrus fruits in jars, you must use ones with hinged glass lids. Try to keep the salt away from the wired metal hinges as well.

Salmon Marinated in Dill (*Gravad Lax*)

Serves 6–8

1.25kg/2¾lb fresh salmon centre cut (see right)

1 very large bunch fresh dill

100g/3½oz/scant ½ cup sea salt

75g/3¾oz/½ cup white caster (superfine) sugar

2 tablespoons white peppercorns, crushed

2 tablespoons vodka

Gravad Lax is easily made at home. It tastes better than shop-bought and is much more economical – what's not to like?

Make sure your salmon is squeaky fresh – I ask for sushi grade at the fishmonger's. You are best with a centre cut, as you need both sides of the salmon with the skin on, but with the backbone and pin bones removed. I cut the tail portions off and use them for other dishes. Naturally, if you have a crowd to feed, you can cure the whole salmon.

Place half the fish, skin-side down, in a shallow dish. Roughly chop the dill and mix with it the salt, sugar and crushed peppercorns. Cover the salmon with this dry cure, pour over the vodka and place the other piece of salmon on top, skin-side up. Cover the fish with clingfilm (plastic wrap) and place a board or plate, slightly bigger than the salmon, on top. Place a weight on top of the plate to press the fish down.

Refrigerate for two days, turning the fish every 12 hours and spooning over the liquid from the salmon. Remember to replace the weight each time.

Remove the salmon from the brine and slice it thinly, across the grain as you would smoked salmon. Serve with a dill mustard sauce (see page 128), and thin slices of good bread lightly buttered.

Dill Mustard Sauce

Serves 6–8

1 tablespoon Dijon mustard

2 tablespoons clear honey

2 tablespoons rice vinegar

1 egg

1 egg yolk

sea salt and freshly ground black pepper

1 small bunch fresh dill

425ml/15fl oz/1¾ cups groundnut oil

Perhaps my favourite part of gravadlax is this mustard sauce. I find that if the sauce doesn't taste quite right, adding extra honey does the trick.

Put the mustard, honey, vinegar, whole egg and egg yolk and a little seasoning into the goblet of a blender and whizz until smooth. Add the dill and whizz for a few seconds.

Now, with the motor running, pour in the oil, very slowly at first then in a thin stream until the mixture thickens. Taste and adjust the seasoning.

While salt is a rather unfashionable ingredient at the moment, a light salting really improves many types of fresh fish. White fish like cod, coley and pollack have a wetter texture than my favourite fish, haddock – salting leaches out some of this moisture and adds a savoury flavour. Thus, texture and taste are improved by this one simple step.

The technique is very simple. As ever, you should use the freshest of fish. The salt chosen can be ordinary table salt, but I tend to use kosher salt or salt crystals as these melt more gently into the fish.

You may salt whole sides or individual portions, but if you use portions of fish, make sure they are cut from the thick end of the fillet. The final few centimetres of the tail end of a whole side will become rather over salty, and may need discarding.

I've added lemon zest to my salt, but crushed pepper, fennel seeds and chilli flakes could all work well.

Once salted, always rinse the fish well and pat it dry before cooking. The fish can be steamed, pan-fried or baked in the oven, when it is especially good roasted on a bed of finely sliced potatoes drizzled with olive oil.

Salting Fresh Fish

Serves 4

1 whole side or 4 thick slices fresh cod,
    skin on, approx. 225g/8oz each
    (cut from the thick end of the fillet)
salt flakes or coarse rock salt
finely grated zest of 1 lemon, or a little
    chopped preserved lemon
    (see page 138)

Wash and trim the fillets as necessary. Feeling the cod carefully with your fingers, locate and remove the pin bones from the centre of the fillets. Lay the fish, skin-side down, in a shallow glass or china dish and, having mixed the salt with the lemon zest, sprinkle this mixture evenly over the fillets. Cover the dish with clingfilm (plastic wrap) and leave in a cool place or the bottom of the fridge for 6 hours.

Roast Salt Cod

Serves 4

4 thick slices home-salted cod
   (see page 129)
olive oil, for frying

This is a wonderful recipe, very simple to do and quite delicious to eat.

Wash the fillets well under running cold water, then pat dry using kitchen paper (paper towels).

Put a heavy non-stick pan on the stove to heat. When the pan is hot, add about 3 tablespoons olive oil and, when that too is hot, put in the fillets, skin-side down. Cook over a high heat until the skin is very crisp and golden, about 6–8 minutes. The fish should be nearly opaque by this time. Turn and cook for a further 1–2 minutes then turn over once more, take the pan from the heat and leave the fish to rest for about 2 minutes.

Serve with mashed potatoes and a lemon butter sauce, or in a bowl of fresh pea soup. I know the latter sounds strange, but it is truly delicious.

A fresh tomato sauce or salsa also works well with this cod dish. Season the sauce with basil, or even coriander, chopped just before serving.

This pork dish reminds me of the Lincolnshire pork butchers of my childhood, and has much in common with lardo, *the exquisite Italian cured pork fat.* Lardo *is dry-cured then hung for six months in an airy barn or outhouse. My version is wet-cured and then cooked before it gets its fresh rosemary topping.*

You must use a slow-grown animal. I choose Gloucester Old Spot or similar, whatever my trusted butcher tells me is good that day.

As this is served in very thin slices, it's best to ask your butcher to bone the belly. I prefer to leave the skin on for cooking, removing it once the pork is cooled. The fat is the point of this dish and you want to keep as much as possible on the joint.

Find a plastic, glass or china dish big enough to hold the pork laid flat and the brine as well.

Place the salt in about 400ml/14fl oz/ 1¾ cups hot water and stir until it has dissolved. Add enough cold water to make up to 2 litres/3½ pints/7 cups. Chill.

Once the brine is cold, place the pork in the dish and pour over the brine. You may need to weight the belly down so it sits fully beneath the liquid. (I place a weight in a ziplock bag and lie this on top.) Now cover the dish with a lid or clingfilm (plastic wrap) and place in the fridge. Leave for 48 hours.

To cook the pork, remove it from the brine and wash under cold water. Place in a saucepan and cover with cold water. Put this on the heat and bring to the boil. When it boils, pour off this water, replacing it with fresh cold water. Bring this to simmering point and cook the pork for 90 minutes or until tender.

Remove the pork from the saucepan and

Cured Salt Pork

Serves 6–8

1kg/2¼lb belly of pork joint
1 tablespoon chopped fresh rosemary
1 teaspoon black peppercorns, crushed

Brine
600g/1lb 5oz/2¾ cups sea salt
2 litres/3½ pints/7 cups water

place on a rack to cool. Discard the cooking liquor. When cool enough to touch, carefully skin the pork, leaving as much fat as possible. Place the cooled pork on a dish, cover with clingfilm and chill for at least 24 hours.

Mix the rosemary and crushed peppercorns on a plate, and roll the top of the joint in this to coat. To serve, cut into thin slices and serve with brown bread and piccalilli, gherkins or mustard fruits (the Italian *mostarda di frutta*).

Roasted Brine-cured Pork

Serves 8–10

2kg/4½lb boneless belly of pork,
 rind on and scored

Brine
90g/3¼oz/¾ cup caster (superfine) sugar
150g/5½oz/½ cup coarse sea salt
15 black peppercorns
8 juniper berries
2 tablespoons fennel seeds
5 sprigs each of fresh rosemary and
 thyme
6 fresh bay leaves

It always seems a little strange to me that soaking pork, or other fatty meats such as goose or duck, that you are about to roast will give a crisper finish, but it does. The osmosis that takes place between the strong brine and the meat means that the fat loses some of its moisture, so roasts more efficiently. And of course you can add lots of good flavours to your brine to enhance the finished dish.

In a large non-metallic container, combine the sugar, salt, peppercorns, juniper berries, fennel seeds, half the rosemary and thyme and all the bay leaves. Add 1 litre/1¾ pints/3½ cups boiling water, stirring to dissolve the sugar and salt completely. Add 3 litres/5¼ pints/10½ cups cold water to cool the brine.

Place the pork in the brine, making sure it is completely submerged. If the meat floats to the surface, weight it down with a plate. Cover and refrigerate. Allow the pork to cure for at least 24–48 hours. The brine will draw out moisture from the meat and accentuate its sweet flavour. A longer curing process will produce a saltier and more pronounced taste from the brine.

Several hours before roasting, remove the pork from the brine and place it on a rack to drain. Allow the meat to come up to room temperature.

Preheat oven to 220°C/425°F/Gas Mark 7.

Dry the pork and place it on a roasting rack in a roasting pan and put it in the centre of the oven to roast until the skin is crackling and brown and the meat begins to exude fat and juices – about 20–30 minutes.

Reduce heat to 150°C/300°F/Gas Mark 2. Continue roasting the pork for 2 hours until meltingly tender. If the skin hasn't 'crackled', place it under a hot grill for 3–4 minutes.

Remove from the oven and rest for 20 minutes before slicing.

Once again, I would suggest serving any salted meat or fish with fairly simple accompaniments. Potato, cooked with a second vegetable such as carrot, parsnip and celeriac and then mashed, works well. Naturally, I would serve a bright green vegetable such as broccoli, Savoy cabbage or Swiss chard, with perhaps apple sauce as a nod to tradition.

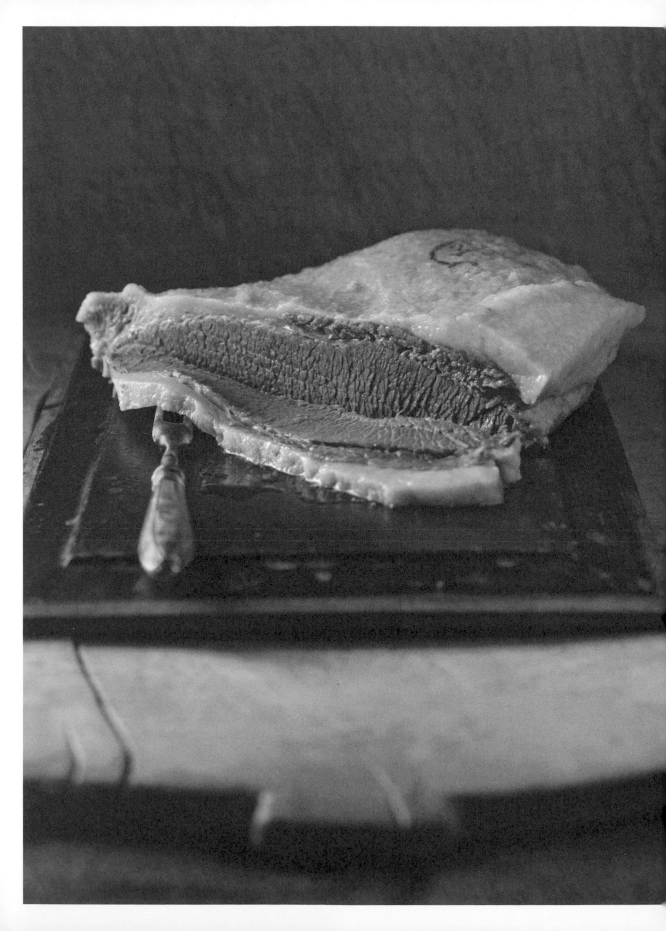

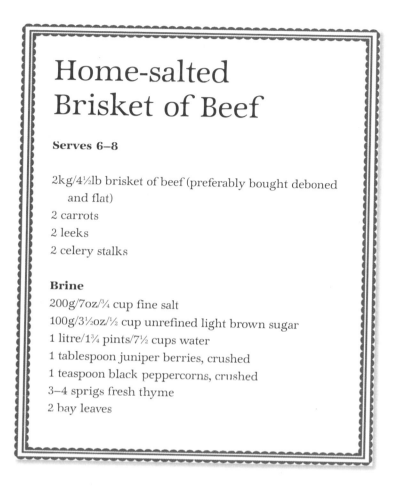

Home-salted Brisket of Beef

Serves 6–8

2kg/4½lb brisket of beef (preferably bought deboned
    and flat)
2 carrots
2 leeks
2 celery stalks

Brine
200g/7oz/¾ cup fine salt
100g/3½oz/½ cup unrefined light brown sugar
1 litre/1¾ pints/7½ cups water
1 tablespoon juniper berries, crushed
1 teaspoon black peppercorns, crushed
3–4 sprigs fresh thyme
2 bay leaves

Home salting gives a really lovely result here, and whilst the meal won't have the pinkish hue that commercially salted meat has, it still looks and tastes wonderful. I use juniper, a spice I love, but you could be as adventurous as you like. Star anise or caraway work well, too.

Mix the salt and sugar in about 250ml/9fl oz/1 cup hot water, stir to dissolve, then add the remaining 750ml/26fl oz/3¼ cups cold water and all the seasonings. Chill.

Lay the brisket in a dish large enough for it to lie flat and deep enough for it to be fully covered by the brine. Pour over the brine and weight the beef down with a dish or plate. The meat must be totally immersed. If you have insufficient brine, make up another batch using the proportions above.

Place in the fridge and leave for five to seven days.

To cook, wash the meat under cold water then place in a large saucepan or casserole. Cover with cold water and bring to the boil. Once boiled, pour off this water and replace with fresh. Add the carrots, leeks and celery stalks and bring back to the boil. Turn the heat to simmer and cook for 2½–3 hours or until very tender.

Serve with suet dumplings (see page 159), spring greens and good hot mustard.

Corned Beef Hash

Serves 4

800g/1¾lb maincrop potatoes, peeled
sea salt and freshly ground black pepper
3 tablespoons olive oil or dripping
1 large onion, peeled and finely chopped
2 celery stalks, finely chopped
1 plump garlic clove, peeled and crushed
1–2 hot red chillies
approx. 300–400g/11–14oz cold salt beef,
    or 1 x 400g/14oz tin corned beef
1–2 tablespoons Worcestershire sauce
a few drops of Tabasco sauce

A serious breakfast or supper favourite, this recipe uses up any leftover salt beef from your boiled beef recipe. If you were so greedy that there were no leftovers, use a can of corned beef, itself a leftover, as corned beef was created as a by-product of the beef-extract industry in Argentina.

I like quite a spicy hash, so use chopped fresh chillies and a good dash of Tabasco. Worcestershire sauce is essential, and I have even added a little freshly grated horseradish…

Boil the potatoes in salted water until tender. Drain, return to the pan and allow to dry over the heat for a few minutes. Reserve.

Heat the oil in a heavy-bottomed frying pan and when hot fry the onion, celery and garlic until soft. Add the chilli and cook for a few minutes more.

Meanwhile, chop the beef into small pieces and add it to the pan. Stir well, breaking the beef down a little with a spatula.

Now add the potato and mash all the ingredients together. Season well with the Worcestershire sauce, Tabasco and some salt and pepper.

Fry the hash turning until everything begins to cook and colour, then, without stirring, fry for a few more moments to give a golden crust on the underside.

Invert the hash carefully on to a plate then slide this gently back into the pan, crust-side up. Cook until the underside, too, is golden.

Serve the hash cut into quarters topped with a fried or poached egg and a good dollop of roasted tomato ketchup (see page 218).

Brining poultry gives it a wonderful flavour. The brine, rather counter-intuitively, makes the meat moister and so more succulent to eat. With richer birds, such as duck and goose, it helps to season the fat and gives an extra crisp finish to the skin, but even with chicken and turkey the skin will still be absolutely delicious.

The brine recipe below works well for a 5kg/12lb goose or turkey. Divide the quantities in half for chicken or duck. I am using Chinese flavourings in this recipe, but for a more traditional flavour use the Brined Pork seasoning on page 132.

In a large, non-metallic container, combine the sugar and sea salt. Add 1 litre/1¾ pints of boiling water and stir until the sugar and salt completely dissolve.

In a pestle and mortar, crush the whole spices together to release their flavours. Add the crushed spices to the brine, along with the orange and lemon zest, the soy sauce and the ginger. Add 3 litres/5 pints of cold water to cool the brine.

Place the bird in the brine, making sure it is completely submerged. If the meat floats to the surface, weight it down with a plate. Cover and refrigerate or place in a very cold larder or outhouse. Allow to cure for 24–48 hours.

About a hour or so before roasting, remove the bird from the brine and place it on a rack to drain, allowing the meat to come up to room temperature.

Pat the skin dry with kitchen paper and make sure you've drained any brine from the body cavity.

Preheat the oven to 220°C/425°F/Gas Mark 7. Place the fruit and onion into the body cavity, then place the bird on a rack over a deep roasting tin and put it into the oven. Cook for 20–30 minutes.

Brined Roast Goose (or Chicken, Turkey or Duck)

5kg/12 lb free-range goose

For the brine:
90g/3¼oz/¾ cup raw (unrefined) sugar
150g/5½oz/½ cup coarse sea salt
1 tablespoon black peppercorns
4–6 star anise, crushed
Grated zest of 1 orange and 1 lemon
200ml/7fl oz/¾ cup dark soy sauce
2-inch piece fresh ginger, coarsely grated

To roast:
1 orange, 1 lemon, 1 apple, 1 onion, all quartered

Reduce the heat to 180°C/350°F/Gas Mark 4. Baste with the juices, adding more chicken stock if necessary (about 125ml/4fl oz/½ cup at a time, to maintain a thin layer of liquid in the pan at all times). Roast for about 4 hours. To check whether the bird is cooked through, insert a skewer into the deepest part of the leg – the juices should run clear.

Preserved Lemons

Fills 2 x 500g/18oz jars

1kg/2¼lb unwaxed lemons
250g/9oz/1 cup cooking salt, plus extra
    as required
bay leaves and whole chillies, to decorate
    (optional)

Salted lemons hail from North Africa where they are used extensively to add depth of flavour to freshly cooked foods such as tagines, couscous and dips. Salted lemons have a profoundly lemony taste, but one that lacks sharpness.

Jars of preserved lemons are very simple to make and look suitably exotic in the kitchen. The downside? Well, you have to wait about three months before they're ready to use. The fact that the lemons take several months to salt means that they have the advantage of age – age being always more interesting than youth (when it come to flavours at least!).

Scrub the lemons under hot water and cut into quarters. Pack these into jars, adding a generous layer of salt between each layer. Push the lemon halves down well, then top up the jars with water. Put on the lids, then gently shake the jar. If all the salt dissolves, open the jar and add more.

Repeat the process each day for two weeks, gently shaking the jar and adding more salt if necessary. You must always be able to see a layer of salt sitting in the bottom of the jar. If you want the preserved lemons to look even prettier, tuck a couple of bay leaves and a chilli down the sides as you layer.

Leave the lemons for two to three months to mature.

To use, take a piece of lemon from the jar and rinse under cold water.

Scrap the centre of the lemon away from the peel and pith. Discard the centre. Finely chop the peel and pith and add to stews, casseroles, mashed potatoes, tagines and sauces.

Spiced Salted Nuts

Makes 250g/9oz

250g/9oz/1½ cups blanched almonds
2 tablespoons olive oil
1 teaspoon raw egg white
1 tablespoon salt flakes, crushed
1 teaspoon cumin seeds, roasted and
    finely ground

I'm using almonds here but cashews, Brazil nuts and walnuts all work well. You can vary the spices to taste, as well – ground roasted cumin is a present favourite, taking over from pimentón de la vera, *that wonderful smoky, hot paprika that is one of the most recognizable flavours of Spain.*

Preheat the oven to 150ºC/300ºF/Gas Mark 2.

Place the almonds on a baking sheet oiled with just enough olive oil to moisten them. Roast in the preheated oven for about 30 minutes until they turn a pale golden brown.

Turn them while hot in the beaten egg white – they will turn glossy.

Then turn them in the salt, which will stick, giving them a slightly salty jacket that dries in the heat. Serve fresh and warm.

The egg white here gives a gloss, but it is not strictly necessary – the oil will work just as well.

Dukkah

Makes 150g/5½oz

100g/3½oz/½ cup shelled hazelnuts,
   walnuts, peanuts or almonds
30g/1oz/scant ¼ cup sesame seeds
15g/½oz/1½ tablespoons coriander seeds
15g/½oz/1½ tablespoons cumin seeds
about 1 teaspoon sea salt flakes
freshly ground black pepper

If you've never eaten dukkah, *let me give you a severe warning: it's worryingly addictive. Salty and spicy, with a flavour rich with roasted nuts,* dukkah *is eaten on bread that has first been dipped into a little extra virgin olive oil. I think that white breads, pitta or ciabatta are the breads of choice here; this is not the place for the wholesome flavour of brown bread.*

Serve dukkah *with pre-dinner drinks.*

Preheat the oven to 200°C/400°F/Gas Mark 6.

Put the nuts on a baking tray and roast them in the preheated oven for 5–10 minutes or until they begin to colour and smell toasted.

Meanwhile put the seeds into a dry frying pan and toast them over a high heat until they, too, begin to smell delicious.

Grind the seeds either in a pestle and mortar or a spice mill to fine crumbs. Whiz the nuts in a food processor until finely chopped. The idea is to form a dry mix, not a paste, so go carefully.

Once crushed, combine the nuts and seeds and add salt and pepper to taste.

Store in an airtight container in a cool place.

RENDERING
AND FATS

Introduction

It seems a little strange that in these times of low-fat diets I should be a powerful advocate of fat, but it is essential that we realize the importance that fat holds in our diets, and recognize how to get it in its best and purest forms.

Our ancestors knew its value and how important fat was for nutrition, for preserving, and a myriad of other household uses. One illustration of this vital role of fats is found in *Miss Parola's New Cookbook: A guide to appetising and healthy food at a reasonable outlay of expense and skill*, written in 1880 by Maria Parola, principal of The School of Cooking, Boston, Mass. In this exhaustive book she fills two long pages telling us of the importance of collecting every scrap of fat, even that bubbling on the surface of stocks and soups, and places much emphasis on the correct way to store it, which fats can be mixed with which, and suggesting that a good larder will have no less than five jars of differing sizes for different types of fat, plus an additional container for saving fat that is to be used for soap-grease. Interestingly, she deems goose and duck fat to be too unpleasant to eat, and therefore destined for the soap pot!

Apart from being a food that has a high calorific value, a virtue much needed in days of manual labour and no central heating, fat contains the essential vitamins A, D, E and K, which maintain healthy skin and bones, plus being imperative to ensure that blood clots effectively. It also tastes good! Why else would we butter toast?

Preserving in fat is common practice and has many merits. There are obviously precautions that need to be taken when keeping meat and vegetables in oil or fat. *Clostridium botulinum* can be a hazard, but if you understand a little about how this rather nasty bug works, all will be well. Essentially, botulism is a problem when preserving foods in a low-acid environment, especially if they have not been heated to boiling point first. So herb oils, for instance, can be a prime suspect. I tend to make such oils fresh, store them in the fridge and use within two weeks. Home-made garlic oil should also be made and used within the week. (Freezing herbs in oil is a good alternative, and even basil will keep well frozen in ice-cube trays chopped fine in olive oil.)

Other bacteria can grow on foods preserved in fat as they will on fresh foods, so salting is often an additional part of the preparation process (see pages 122–125). The rule is that if you are worried about something, always err on the side of caution.

The Variety of Fats

There are many types of fat used in preserving and for cooking, and I have covered most of them here.

'Rendering' is the term used for melting the fat to separate it from the connective tissue that holds it. I think home rendering has fallen out of favour because, before the days of adequate kitchen extraction, the smell of the fat as it melts permeates the whole house. I had lodgings for several weeks where the lady of the house earned extra money by rendering dripping for the local butcher. My clothes smelt for weeks after I had found a new place to stay. Don't let this put you off – after all, she was rendering industrial quantities of dripping!

I have not mentioned schmaltz, the chicken fat widely used in Jewish cuisine, but not usually rendered outside orthodox families. If you want to render schmaltz, the methods for duck or goose fat work well, but you will need a bird from the butcher, as supermarket birds have little or no body fat remaining when they are sold.

Store rendered fat in spotlessly clean glass jars. The old-fashioned dripping bowl, when any cooking fat was poured in, topping up the dish week on week, I find rather suspect. I do like to make sure that beef and pork fat are stored separately. I allow mutton or lamb fat to cool, then discard it.

Goose and Duck Fat

The Dordogne region of France is renowned for its geese and ducks. Grown on small farms, these birds are force-fed grain to cause the livers to swell. The livers are taken for foie gras, the breasts for magret and the rest of the birds, which are wonderfully fatty, are made into confit and rillettes, magnificent dishes that are both cooked and preserved in fat. The meat is salted first to remove some of the excess liquid, then poached covered in fat until the meat is cooked. One of the side benefits of cooking in fat is that meat becomes meltingly tender.

If you roast a goose or duck, do make sure you keep the fat to use in a dozen dishes later. Any raw fat pulled from the carcass before roasting can be rendered in just the same way as you render beef or pork fat (see page 158). The fat spooned from the roasting tin will be darker in colour but still excellent in flavour. When using fat from the roasting tin, you should pour the fat into a small bowl, let it go cold, then lift it from the collected jellied juices underneath. You can use these juices in soups or stews. Melt the fat until bubbling, then pour into a hot sterilized jar, covering with a lid.

You can now buy jars and tins of goose and duck fat in supermarkets, which is wonderful. Potatoes roasted in this are quite simply the best. Once you have opened a tin, pour any excess fat into a glass jar and cover with a lid. The fat left in the pan after the vegetables have been roasted can be added to the jar, cooled and stored in the fridge or a cold pantry.

Lard and Dripping

Lard and dripping were once the cooking fats of choice in Britain. Rendered on farms and in homes nationwide, such fats formed the basis of British baking. Whether home-rendered or bought from a local butcher, these fats had integrity. Pure and simple, they were the melted fat of beef cattle (dripping) or of pork (lard). No emulsifiers, no transfats, no spooky chemistry, you simply put the raw animal fat in a pan over a low heat, cook it gently for a couple of hours and you have a wonderful supply of fat for use in almost all your recipes. I give you details of how to render both lard and dripping on page 158.

Suet is the hardest of animal fats and comes from the area around cattle and sheep kidneys, where it serves to protect these vital organs. Suet is usually used in its raw state (see page 158), but it can be rendered just as the other fats.

Butter

Not strictly speaking a fat to be rendered, but butter is used in much the same way as the other fats in potting. Potting of fish, meat and cheese is one of the oldest preservation methods. At first in Britain, it was suet that was used: the food was cooked, shredded or not, placed in a pot and then liquid suet poured over to make it airtight when set. A sort of medieval clingfilm (plastic wrap). By Tudor times, the suet had been replaced with butter. I have given three potted fish recipes here, but you could also pot herring, salmon and trout – in fact, most oily fish. Another old English tradition was the making of fish pastes, a very different animal to the potted fish paste commercially sold as sandwich filling. These early pastes contained almost exactly the same ingredients and seasonings as potted fish, but were pounded to make them smooth enough to spread. These, too, would be packed in sterilized glass or china pots and covered with clarified butter to seal out the air.

Potted meat was originally covered with a flour and water paste, or a thick layer of suet. Today, potted meat is made on the same principle and for the same uses as the French pâtés and terrines, the consistency being either paste-like or coarse. Clarified butter is used for the airtight covering. An interesting cultural difference between French pâté and British potted meat is that the former is considered to be a high-end dish, and the latter the food of the working class.

Clarified Butter

Clarified butter is butter that has been heated to rid it of the water and dairy solids that remain in the butter after it has been churned. Because this butter is to be used to seal dishes from the air, it needs to be pure fat.

❖ Place the butter you wish to clarify in a pan (I find a stainless steel one best). Put the pan over a gentle heat and allow the butter to melt.

❖ Now you must skim any scum that is on the surface of the butter and discard it. Let the butter simmer for a few minutes; at first it will be frothy, then the bubbles will die down. This simmering boils off the water from the butter. Let the butter cool for a few minutes then pour the golden yellow fat carefully out of the pan into a clean dish, leaving behind the milk solid which will have settled on the bottom of the pan.

❖ Clarified butter keeps well and has the added advantage of having a higher burn point than unclarified butter, so it can be used for frying.

❖ Ghee is a form of clarified butter often found in Asian markets.

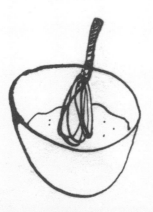

Potted Shrimps

Serves 4–6 as a starter

1.2 litres/2 pints tiny brown shrimps
225g/8oz/2 sticks butter
a little lemon juice
Tabasco sauce
freshly grated nutmeg
sea salt and freshly ground black pepper

Peeling a pile of tiny brown shrimps is a real labour of love, but the result more than compensates for the effort. Alternatively, buy ready-peeled shrimps from your fish merchant. You can, of course, use supermarket prawns in this recipe, but they have a lighter flavour, so zizz them up with extra Tabasco and lemon zest.

Peel the shrimps. (The shells can be saved and used to make a fish stock.)

In a pan, melt the butter, adding a few drops of lemon juice, a good shake of Tabasco, some nutmeg, salt and pepper. Taste to ensure the butter is well seasoned and the flavours balance – when cold, the flavours will be less pronounced. Add the shrimps and cook them gently in the butter for 1 minute.

Pour the mixture into a small dish or divide between ramekins and leave to set. (Potted shrimps can be topped with clarified butter – see page 147 – to give an airtight seal.)

Serve as a starter or with salad leaves as a light lunch with crusty brown bread. I also love to serve a ramekin of potted shrimps spooned into the centre of a jacket potato for supper – delicious. You could also gently warm the shrimps and use them as a simple sauce for fish – perhaps the roasted salt cod on page 130.

Keep in the fridge or a very cold larder for up to one week.

Potted Crab

Serves 4

225g/8oz crab meat (the meat from
   1 large or 2 medium crabs)
55g/2oz/½ stick butter
finely grated zest and juice of 1 lemon
Tabasco sauce
freshly grated nutmeg
sea salt and freshly ground black pepper
1 tablespoon finely chopped fresh parsley
   or even basil

Many people don't like the brown top shell meat of a crab, which I think is due to its rather soft texture and slightly stronger taste. But the brown meat is wonderful, and, mixed in this recipe, gives a depth of flavour that the white meat on its own can never achieve.

Make sure the crab meat is completely free of little pieces of shell. Mix white and brown together.

In a pan, melt the butter, adding the lemon zest and a few drops of juice, a good shake of Tabasco, some nutmeg, salt and pepper, and herbs. Taste to ensure the butter is well seasoned and the flavours balance, as, when cold, the flavours will be less pronounced. Add the crab and cook it gently in the butter for 1 minute.

Pour the mixture into a small dish or divide between ramekins and leave to set.

Serve as a starter or light lunch with salad leaves and crusty brown bread. I also like to serve potted crab on little pieces of toast or crostini as a canapé.

Keep for up to seven days in the fridge.

Some oriental seasoning works well here, grated fresh ginger perhaps, teamed with fresh coriander (cilantro) or maybe just a pinch of ground star anise.

This is a wonderful way of making a luxury ingredient go a long way. Serve the lobster at room temperature with good old-fashioned Melba toast (see below) and some lemon wedges.

Pick over the lobster meat to make sure there are no small pieces of shell.

In a pan, melt the butter, adding the lemon zest, chilli, chives, some nutmeg, salt and pepper. Taste to ensure that the butter is well seasoned and the flavours balance, as, when cold, the flavours will be less pronounced. Add the lobster and cook it gently in the butter for 1 minute only.

Pour the mixture into a small dish or divide between ramekins and leave to set. Chill until about 1 hour before you serve.

Serve as a starter with Melba toast or spread on a cocktail canapé.

Potted Lobster

Serves 4–6

225g/8oz lobster meat
55g /2oz/½ stick butter
finely grated zest of 1 lemon
1–2 hot red chillies, chopped
2 tablespoons chopped fresh chives
freshly grated nutmeg
sea salt and freshly ground black pepper

Strangely, I find that the best bread for Melba toast is supermarket sliced white! Choose one that has been thickly sliced and, if you can, one that's a few days old.

Toast both sides of the bread in a toaster or under the grill until a mid-gold in colour.

Allow the toast to cool until you can touch it, then cut off the crusts. Carefully split the rounds of toast open through the middle, giving you two thin pieces toasted on one side only.

Lay the 'toasts' on a baking sheet and place in a low oven (140ºC/320ºF/ Gas Mark 1) and cook until dry and crisp – about 60 minutes.

Allow to cool fully before storing in an airtight tin, for up to three months.

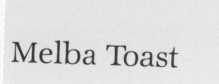

Melba Toast

Confit Salmon & Salmon Rillettes

Serves 4–6

500g/18oz fresh salmon fillet, skinned
250ml/9fl oz strained duck fat

Rillettes
1 teaspoon finely grated lemon zest
2 tablespoons chopped fresh coriander
 (cilantro) (optional)
sea salt and freshly ground black pepper
6 drops Tabasco sauce

Simmering fish in duck fat might seem a little odd, but the end result is delicious. The cooked salmon can be served simply with steamed new potatoes, or the recipe can be taken further, as with these rillettes.

Preheat the oven to 150ºC/300ºF/Gas Mark 2.

If making salmon confit, cut the salmon into portions. If making salmon rillettes, cut the salmon into chunks.

Melt the duck fat in a suitable pan. Place the prepared salmon in a shallow pan – a small square cake tin might suit – and cover with melted duck or goose fat. Place in the preheated oven and cook for 1 hour.

Lift the salmon from the fat and, if you have made salmon confit, serve it while still warm.

If making rillettes, place the salmon chunks in a bowl. Pull into flakes using a fork. Now add the lemon zest and coriander (cilantro), about 2 tablespoons of the duck fat and seasoning: salt, pepper and Tabasco. Taste to make sure the seasoning is robust, then pot into either individual ramekins or a deep dish.

Chill for about an hour, then spoon over enough melted duck fat to cover the rillettes by about 5mm/¼in. Store in the fridge for up to one week.

Rillettes de Canard

Serves 4–6

1 whole duck, about 1.5kg/3lb 5oz,
   breasts saved for another recipe
sea salt and freshly ground black pepper
150ml/5fl oz/scant ¾ cup chicken stock
150ml/5fl oz/scant ¾ cup dry white wine
1 bay leaf, crushed
1 teaspoon fresh thyme leaves
1 large garlic clove, peeled and crushed
2 shallots, peeled and chopped
½ teaspoon star anise, crushed
2 tablespoons brandy

Traditionally, rillettes are made from the carcasses of ducks fattened for foie gras. Thrifty French housewives make sure every part of such a valuable bird is used: the breast for magret, the legs for confit, all the fat is rendered, the gizzards potted and the carcasses roasted or boiled to yield their meat for this rich spread. I suggest buying a large duck, cutting off the breast for another use and then continuing as below.

If you do not have sufficient fat, use some bought goose or duck fat.

Preheat the oven to 150°C/300°F/Gas Mark 2.

Trim all the fat and skin from the duck, cut into small pieces and place in a deep frying pan or similar with 3 tablespoons of water. Place this over a low heat and cook gently until the fat begins to render. The water will evaporate and the fat will gently spit until it is liquid, with the remains of the skin crisp. Strain the fat into a jug. (There will be a few crispy bits of skin left, which are delicious to eat.)

Chop the duck carcass and legs into pieces and place them in a roasting dish along with the fat, a teaspoon each of salt and pepper, the stock, wine, herbs, garlic, shallots and star anise. Add about 75ml/2½fl oz/⅓ cup water then cook, covered with foil, in the preheated low oven until the meat is falling off the bone, about 2–3 hours.

Strain, allow to cool, then pick all the lean meat from the bones. Reserve the fat and any juices.

Blend the cooked shallot, garlic and herbs with the brandy and about 200ml/ 7fl oz/⅓ cup of fat and juices. Mix this with the finely shredded meat and season well – it should be very peppery.

Spoon the rillettes into ramekins or a terrine, and cover with a little extra fat. Serve on French bread or brioche.

Keep for two weeks in the fridge.

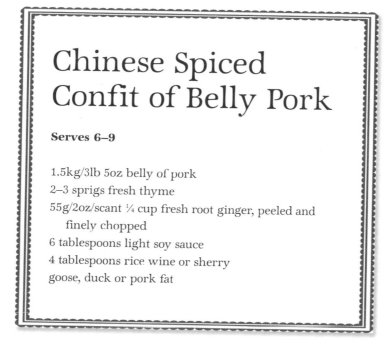

Chinese Spiced Confit of Belly Pork

Serves 6–9

1.5kg/3lb 5oz belly of pork
2–3 sprigs fresh thyme
55g/2oz/scant ¼ cup fresh root ginger, peeled and
 finely chopped
6 tablespoons light soy sauce
4 tablespoons rice wine or sherry
goose, duck or pork fat

This is a rather Chinese way of cooking pork, but with a French twist.

You marinate the pork for 24 hours then simmer it in fat. To serve, you reheat the pork in a hot oven (200°C/400°F/Gas Mark 6) for 20 minutes. I like it either on mashed potatoes or pulled apart and piled on shredded bitter salad leaves, crisp, slightly oriental salad vegetables or on hot spicy egg noodles.

Ask your butcher to bone the pork and cut it into 10cm/4in squares. You will get either six or nine.

Mix the marinade ingredients together and rub them well into the meat. Place in a china dish or bowl and cover with clingfilm (plastic wrap). Leave the meat to marinate in the fridge for at least 24 hours.

Preheat the oven to 150°C/300°F/Gas Mark 2.

Lift the meat from the marinade and pat dry with kitchen paper (paper towels). Place the cubes of pork in a roasting or other ovenproof dish just big enough to hold them in a single layer. The dish should be deeper than the meat as next you are going to cover the pork with melted fat.

Place the dish in the oven and cook for 3 hours. The meat should be very tender and pull apart if touched.

Carefully lift the meat from the fat and place in a spotlessly clean glass dish, again in a single layer. Spoon over enough hot fat to cover, being careful to avoid any of the juices in the pan, as these will cause the meat to spoil. Cover with clingfilm and store in the fridge for up to three months.

Confit of Duck

Makes 6–8 pieces

about 6–8 raw duck legs
1 large tin duck or goose fat, or
    1k/2¼lb/4½ cups lard

Marinade
2–4 tablespoons brandy
6 tablespoons salt
freshly ground black pepper
fresh thyme leaves

Whilst ducks only come with two legs, this recipe takes a little time, so I use as many legs as I can find. The confit keeps well in the fridge and makes such easy and luxurious meals.

Place the duck legs in a china or glass bowl and pour on the brandy. Rub well with the salt, pepper and thyme leaves, cover with clingfilm (plastic wrap) and leave somewhere cool overnight.

Preheat the oven to 150ºC/300ºF/Gas Mark 2.

Next scrape off the salt and herbs and place the legs skin-side down in an ovenproof and heatproof pan large enough to hold them in a single layer. Cook the legs over a gentle heat until the fat starts to run, then turn up the heat and cook for a few minutes to colour the skin. Turn them skin-side up, and add enough melted goose fat, duck fat or lard to almost cover. Put the pan back on the heat and bring up to a gentle simmer. Place the pan in the preheated low oven, and allow the confit to cook for about 2½ hours.

Once the confit has cooled a little, lift the legs into a deep china dish or bowl. Pour the fat into a saucepan, trying to leave any duck juices behind. Heat the fat and then pour enough over the legs to cover them. Store the remaining fat in a sterilized glass jar with a lid (duck fat is liquid gold, and makes the best roast potatoes). Store the confit duck in a cool place for up to three months. There is always a slight possibility of mould developing, so make sure your dishes and jars are spotlessly clean (see page 165) and that as much of the cooking juices as possible are removed before potting.

To serve, lift as many legs as you need from the fat, and arrange on a baking sheet. Cook in a hot oven (200ºC/400ºF/Gas Mark 6) for 15 minutes or until crisp. Serve with red cabbage or a green vegetable, like chard or spinach and mashed potatoes.

Rendering Your Own Lard and Beef Dripping

> 2kg/4½lb raw beef or pork fat
> 200ml/7fl oz/¾ cup water

Home-rendered beef dripping is the most wonderfully flavoursome fat. I keep a jar for cooking Yorkshire puddings, for cooking the onions for a rich French onion soup, and for adding depth of flavour to a myriad of stews and casseroles.

Lard is the fat of choice for pig farmers, and any housewife who keeps a couple of pigs on a smallholding. Lard is the most wonderfully useful fat, with a milder taste than dripping. I love to use lard in pastry but also when making biscuits, baked puddings and, of course, pork pies.

It's difficult to say just how much dripping you will get from each kg/2¼lb of fat. I find, though, that pork fat (lard) gives less fat than beef. This, I think, is the result of our farmers' continuing search for ever-leaner pigs. You might try asking an organic butcher for outdoor-reared traditional bred pork, but I mostly find that fat from these treasured beasts is hard to get hold of.

It's worth getting at least 2kg/4½lb of raw fat as the process takes much the same amount of time, no matter how much you make.

Chop the fat into pieces about 5cm/2in in size. Place these in a deep frying pan and add the water. Place the pan over a low heat and gently heat the water. As the water simmers the fat will start to melt. Keep the pan over the heat until all the water evaporates. Keep the heat low and continue to cook the fat until all the connective tissue that holds the fat is left as little crackling-like pieces in the bottom of the pan.

Strain the fat through a fine mesh sieve, then pour it into spotlessly clean jars. Cover with screw-on lids and allow the fat to cool. Store in the fridge or a cold larder. Beef dripping or lard keeps well for three months or more.

Don't throw away the crispy pieces in the bottom of the pan, as they make a delicious snack (especially with a glass of cider). Spoon them on to kitchen paper (paper towels) to drain, and then sprinkle with a little coarse salt.

Fresh Suet

Fresh suet, the fat taken from around the kidneys of cattle and sheep, is available from most butchers. It gives a wonderful flavour and lightness to suet pastry in all manner of puddings or pies, to dumplings (see right) and steamed puddings such as spotted dick (see page 94). Whilst you can buy suet in packets, once you have tried fresh suet, you will be hooked. The fat itself is harder than other fat so can be finely chopped and mixed into flour very easily, with no rubbing in. Mutton suet has a stronger flavour than beef and is most suitable for savoury dishes. Beef suet works well in both sweet and savoury recipes.

Take about 300g/10½oz fresh beef suet and chill for several hours.

Over a bowl, carefully pull the solid fat away from the membrane. You will need to take a little care with this, but it's fairly straightforward. Once you have removed as much membrane as possible, grate the fat either using a coarse hand grater or the coarse blade of a food processor. Alternatively, the suet can be finely chopped.

Handling the grated suet carefully, toss in about 2 tablespoons plain (all-purpose) flour.

Store the prepared suet in the fridge for up to one week.

Simple Suet Dumplings

Serves 4–6

150g/5½oz/1½ cups plain (all-purpose) flour
1 teaspoon baking powder
a good pinch of salt
freshly ground black pepper
75g/2¾oz prepared fresh suet
1 tablespoon of chopped fresh parsley, or 1 teaspoon caraway seeds, crushed
4–8 tablespoons cold water, to mix (see below)

Savoury or sweet, these dumplings are lightness itself. The important point here is to make sure the dough is very soft. It should be wet enough to fall off the spoon in the case of a savoury dumpling; a sweet dumpling mix needs to be a little drier if you wish to wrap the dough around fruit like apricots or plums. (Sweet dumplings can be made by leaving out the pepper and seasonings, and adding chopped dates. Serve sprinkled with demerara sugar.)

Mix the dry ingredients and flavourings together. Mix to a soft dough with the water.

Have a pan of water boiling on the heat and drop in tablespoons of the mixture. Simmer over a low heat for about 4–5 minutes. To check if the dumplings are cooked, drain one and slice it open. It should be light and fluffy inside.

Serve at once with stews and casseroles.

JAMS, JELLIES
AND SWEET
PRESERVES

Introduction

Making Jams, Jellies and Preserves

My passion for jam-making started young. With legs still scratched and bleeding from picking raspberries, strawberries and gooseberries, I would pick over the fruit and then help my mother turn it into jars of jewel-bright jams and jellies with which to fill our larder shelves.

We were making a virtue out of a necessity in those far-off post-war years, and you might wonder whether, in these days of farmers' markets, small producers and high-end delis, making your own jam is still worthwhile.

I would say an emphatic yes. Home-made preserves such as jams, jellies, curds and preserved fruit are more than special – they taste delicious, give a wonderful sense of satisfaction, they are a link with everyone in years past who ever gleaned and preserved food, and they will amaze and delight your family.

There are a few simple rules and techniques that will help get you off to a good start.

Fruit

Only make jams with top-quality fruit. This rule really applies to all preserving, but with jam it is especially important. Fruit is at its peak in flavour when just ripe, but many fruits lose acidity when overripe, and it's the correct balance of acidity, sugar and pectin that allows you to achieve a good, easy set. It really doesn't matter where you get your fruit from, whether garden, allotment, farmers' market or supermarket. Just look for firm ripe berries, stone fruit that are highly scented but unbruised, and fresh juicy citrus. One thing to avoid at all costs is fruit marked 'berries for jam'. These will usually be a mix of hard unripe or bruised overripe berries, neither of which make good jam.

Most fruits are good for jam-making once you have understood the process. The idea is simply to cook fruit and sugar together for the shortest possible time to achieve a set. The boiling process eliminates much of the water found naturally in the fruit, and this allows the sugar to act successfully as a preservative. Obviously, fruit with a high water content will need longer boiling than more condensed fruits.

Another point to consider is how the fruit cooks. Apples will need a longer time to break down than, say, raspberries, so a little extra simmering is needed. Small hard-skinned berries, currants, blueberries and cranberries, for example, need cooking until tender before any sugar is added.

Once you have bought your fruit, you need to prepare it. I prefer not to wash berries unless they are very dusty. If you do need to rinse, then allow them to drain on a clean tea towel (dish towel).

I peel stone fruit, such as peaches and apricots, before I use them. To do this, drop the whole fruit into boiling water for a few minutes before removing and slipping off their skins. Then halve to remove the stones and chop the flesh into an appropriate size. Apples and pears will need peeling and coring in the usual fashion. I have recently been using tropical fruit to make preserves, and these I prepare as I would if I were going to eat them fresh.

I like to cut large fruit into cubes of about 1cm/½in. This size I find works well in the finished preserve, giving good-sized chunks on toast or as a cake filling.

The standard recipe for jam is that you use 450g/1lb/2¼ cups of sugar for each 450g/1lb/3 cups fruit. For jellies, the proportions are 450g/1lb/2⅓ cups of sugar to every 600ml/1 pint/2 cups of juice.

The Magic Ingredients for Setting Sugar

The 'set' in jams and jellies is brought about by getting three things in the right proportions: acidity, sugar and pectin.

I have found that almost any white sugar works well when making preserves. There are three main types.

Granulated sugar This medium crystal sugar can be processed from either cane or beet and is the least costly to use. Golden granulated is made from raw cane sugar and, whilst it has a lovely flavour, I find it too strong for jam-making (although it is good for marmalades).

Caster (superfine) sugar This is a fine crystal sugar. Again it can be made either from cane or beet, but is more costly than granulated sugar. It, too, can be made from raw cane sugar, and the same flavour consideration applies.

Preserving sugar This very large crystal sugar, as its name suggests, is sold for jam- and preserve-making. It dissolves easily and is said to reduce scum forming on the jam during the cooking process. Preserving sugar is the most costly of the options and, in practice, I find it an unnecessary expense. I have used granulated sugar for all the preserves in this book with no problems.

'Sugar for jam' The final sugar option is a mix of sugar and pectin which allows an easy set. I tend not to use this sugar, as, once you understand jam-making it's better to add your own pectin if needed in the correct quantity. I sometimes use it, though, when making marmalade with sweet oranges.

Pectin

Pectin is the *wünderkind* of jam-making, for it is really pectin that makes jam set. When combined in the correct ratio with sugar and acid, pectin forms a gel that goes firm when cold.

Many fruits are naturally high in pectin: apples, plums, gooseberries, redcurrants, blackcurrants and quince are the most common. Citrus fruit are high in both acid and pectin, so are very useful in the jam-making process, particularly marmalades. Fruits low in pectin include berries like strawberries, blueberries and blackberries. Stone fruit, including apricots, peaches and cherries and most tropical fruit except guava, are also low in pectin.

As pectin is essential to achieve the set, it must be added to jams when necessary, so you may need to use a commercial brand of prepared pectin. This comes in two forms: either as a powder or a liquid. Both come with full instructions and should be used accordingly. Pectin is available in most supermarkets.

You can, of course, combine low- and high-pectin fruits such as blackberry and apple, gooseberries and strawberries or redcurrants and blueberries to give a good result.

Acid

The third part of the trinity is acidity. It is not always necessary to add extra acidity to jams and jellies. For instance, when using very tart fruit like gooseberries, no extra acidity needs to be added. A simple rule is to taste the fruit, and if it is as sharp as lemon juice, no extra needs adding.

As you can imagine, most fruits do need extra acidity, and this is usually added as lemon juice. An alternative I now use is citric acid, which is easily obtained at food grade and is simple to use. A general rule is that a level tablespoon of citric acid powder gives the same acidity as the juice of one lemon. While some chemists do stock citric acid, I usually buy it from shops which specialize in home brewing. If there is not one near you, the Internet has a host to choose from.

❁❧❧❁

As a footnote, you can make excellent wine jellies, using sugar, acid and pectin. The usual proportions are (for each bottle of wine) 750g/1lb 10oz/2½ cups sugar, juice of 2 lemons, and 1 sachet powdered or 150ml/5fl oz liquid pectin.

Equipment

You need very little special equipment.

For cooking my jams and preserves, I use a large, enamelled, cast-iron casserole dish. You need a pan about 15–20cm/6–8in deep, and one that is also wide enough to give a large surface area: this makes the boiling process as quick as possible, allowing a rapid evaporation of water. Preserving pans work well but are an unnecessary expense unless you are intending to make industrial quantities of jam. If you are nervous about something like a curd 'scrambling', you could use a double boiler instead of an open pan.

You will need a long metal spoon to stir the jam, and several small plates or saucers in the freezer with which to test for a set. A slotted spoon is useful to skin any scum from the surface of the boiling jam.

Jam jars with lids are best, though you can use wax discs and cellophane seals in the more traditional manner. Both jars, lids and seals can be bought from home-ware companies, but I save pretty-shaped jars with their lids ready to use again.

A jam funnel will be of tremendous use when filling the jars. For marmalade, you will also need a square of muslin, in which to tie up the pips and pith, and, of course, you will need a jelly bag if you are planning to make a jelly – along with some way to support it over the bowl into which it will drip.

Sterilizing

Everything to be used in preserve-making – jams, marmalades, pickles and condiments – needs to be spotlessly clean and should be sterilized before use. A dishwasher does this effortlessly, but a good scrub in hot soapy water works just as well. If you've washed glass jars, for instance, a spell thereafter in a hot oven – about 20 minutes at 160ºC/320ºF/Gas Mark 3 – will make sure any bacteria have been dealt with. Taken straight from the dishwasher, this stage can be omitted. Lids have to be sterilized as well, as do all the other pieces of equipment, such as spoons, ladles, funnels, etc.

Cooking Your Jam

The prepared fruit, lemon juice if needed, and sugar are placed in the pan and gently heated. You must stir from time to time until the sugar has dissolved. (This is not true for marmalade, though, see page 175.)

Then, to get the freshest flavour with the quickest set, the jam should be cooked over a high heat for as short a time as possible. The jam should boil rapidly but must be stirred occasionally to ensure the jam doesn't catch.

Testing for a Set

Once the jam or marmalade has been boiling for the time given in the recipe, you will need to start testing for the set. You can tell with a little experience when this point is near: looking at the jam, the boil becomes more sluggish (the bubbles will 'plop' rather than froth), and a spoon of the jam cooled slightly then tipped back into the pot begins to hold together.

The most efficient way to test for the set is to take a chilled plate from the freezer and drop a teaspoon of mixture on to it. Wait a couple of minutes for the jam to cool, then begin pushing the edge of the mound of jam. If a skin has formed and the jam wrinkles, it's ready. If the jam is still liquid it is not ready, so return the pan to the heat and boil rapidly, testing as above every 2–3 minutes. *You must take the jam off the heat while you test for a set. And now that you are so near setting point, stir the mixture often to prevent it sticking and so burning.*

Potting and Labelling

Once you are happy that your jam or jelly has reached setting point, you will need to proceed with potting while it is still hot. I usually leave the jam to settle for about 5 minutes before potting, as this makes the whole process a little safer.

Have ready your clean sterilized jars and lids, funnel and ladle. The jars should be hot when filled with the preserve, so place them on a baking sheet in the oven heated to 160ºC/320ºF/Gas Mark 3 for 15 minutes.

I take the hot jars on the tray and place them close to the preserving pan. Using the jam funnel – or you could pour the jam or marmalade from a jug – fill the jars with the hot mixture, leaving about 1.5cm/⅝in headspace. Try not to dribble the mixture round the top of the jar.

If using wax discs, place these on the hot jam at once, then cover with the cellophane covers. If using lids, place them on the hot jars, and then tighten later once the jars are cool.

Do label your jars clearly, to avoid problems later. You might think you'll remember what jam is in which jar but, trust me, you won't!

For instance, some chutneys can look remarkably like jam... You'll need to write on the name of the preserve, plus the date it was made. (You can get very pretty labels from mail-order outlets and some stores, or you can just use plain ones from stationers.)

Storing

Store your jams, jellies and marmalades in the larder or pantry in wonderful serried rows where you will be able to admire your handiwork. If you have a cold room – even a garage – this will also work well. Some of the preserves in this chapter are best kept in the fridge.

Red Plum Jam

Fills 6 medium (300ml/10fl oz) jars

1kg/2¼lb red plums
250ml/9fl oz/1 cup water
900g/2lb/4¾ cups white sugar

Red jam is much more appealing than yellow jam. This statement is easily proved by watching people choose jam at the breakfast tables in hotels and bed and breakfasts. It seems not to matter what the flavour of the jam is – red is best. I am quite fond of apricot jam, but I know it would seem wrong in a jam roly-poly, and imagine a Victoria sponge sandwich with a yellow filling!

The good news here is that plum jam is the simplest to make, and plums are usually in ready supply, so are cheap. What more could you want!

Cut the plums into halves or quarters, depending on size. As you do this, remove the stones and discard them.

Place the prepared fruit in a preserving pan and add the water. Place the pan over a moderate heat and, stirring gently, cook until the fruit has softened, about 20 minutes.

Now add the sugar, and continue to cook, stirring, until the sugar has dissolved. Turn up the heat and boil rapidly until the jam tests positive for a set (see page 166). Begin testing after 5 minutes; the jam will take about 5–10 minutes to reach this point.

Pot into hot sterilized jars and cover and label in the usual way (see page 166). Keeps for a year.

Store-cupboard Apricot Jam

Fills 1 large (500ml/18fl oz) jar

225g/8oz/1½ cups ready-to-eat dried
   apricots
600ml/1 pint/2 cups water
grated zest and juice of 1 lime
225g/8oz/scant 1¼ cups white sugar
¼ teaspoon cardamom seeds, crushed
   (optional)

If you suddenly get the urge for a jar of home-made jam, this is the recipe for you. It's easy to make, uses store-cupboard ingredients, and is sure to set well. If only life was that simple...

If you want to use cardamom and have bought cardamom pods, these must be crushed and the tiny black seeds removed. These seeds should then be crushed further. Discard the remains of the pods.

Put the apricots into a pan with the water, and bring to a slow simmer. Cook, with the pan covered, until the fruit is soft – about 15 minutes.

Now remove the lid, add the lime zest and juice and sugar and cook over a low heat until the sugar has dissolved. Turn up the heat and boil until thick – about a further 20 minutes.

Stir in the crushed cardamom seeds, if using, then pot into hot sterilized jars and cover and label in the usual way (see page 166). Keeps for three months.

This jam is wonderful on hot buttered scones and makes a wonderful sponge filling, stirred into whipped cream.

Summer Fruit Jam

Fills 1 large (500ml/18fl oz) jar

1kg/2¼lb/6¾ cups mixed summer fruit:
the bigger the mix the better, but
include strawberries (hulled and
halved if large), raspberries and
blackcurrants, stringed
juice of 2 large lemons
900g/2lb/4½ cups white sugar

The berries for this jam could come from a number of places. A garden is the first and obvious choice, but I made a batch this year using some berries I had left from a visit to the pick-your-own farm. I've even found a couple of punnets of supermarket ready-mixed berries in my fridge that I've cooked up. Do try and have some gooseberries, topped and tailed, or redcurrants, stringed, in the mix as these will help the jam set. A handful of pitted cherries add texture, but don't add too many as cherries have little of the all-important pectin. Blueberries work well as do chopped red plums, if you're a little short on weight.

Mix the prepared fruit in a preserving pan and add the lemon juice. Put over a low heat and stir gently until the fruit gives up some of its juice – about 10 minutes. If you use blueberries, these must soften before you add the sugar.

Once the fruit is soft, add the sugar and stir over a low heat until this has dissolved. Turn up the heat and boil rapidly until you reach setting point (see page 166), about 5 or so minutes.

Pot into hot sterilized jars, cover and label in the usual way (see page 166). Keeps for up to three months.

Is there anyone who doesn't love strawberry jam? So, why then is it the most difficult jam of them all to make? I have, over the years, tried many different recipes, all of them trying to capture the fresh taste of the berries, while getting a decent enough set for the preserve to balance on a scone and not drip down your chin.

This recipe is the one I am using now. It works a treat, giving a well-set jam with a fresh zingy taste. I've used citric acid to give the much-needed acidity to the mix. Don't be frightened of using this, it's really the same as lemon juice, but in an easier and more measurable form.

Strawberry Jam

Fills 4 medium (300ml/10fl oz) jars

1kg/2¼lb/6¾ cups small ripe strawberries
I kg/2¼lb/5 cups white sugar
2 level teaspoons citric acid
125ml/4fl oz/⅓ cup liquid pectin

Placed the hulled berries in a large stainless-steel or enamelled preserving pan.

Mix the sugar and citric acid together and sprinkle this over the berries. Leave for about 2 hours, stirring occasionally. The strawberries will begin to give off some of their juice.

Place the pan over a low heat and cook, stirring often, until the sugar has completely dissolved and there is no grittiness remaining. Stir in the pectin.

Bring the mixture to the boil and boil over a high heat for 3–4 minutes. Turn off the heat and test for a set (see page 166). If the setting point has not been reached, continue to boil, testing every 2 minutes. The jam should take no longer than 8–10 minutes.

Allow to cool for 30 minutes before potting into hot sterilized jars and sealing in the usual manner (see page 166). Keeps for six months.

Blackcurrant Jam

Fills 2–3 large (500ml/18fl oz) jars

1kg/2¼lb/6¾ cups blackcurrants
1 litre/1¾ pints/3½ cups water
1.25kg/2¾lb/6½ cups white sugar

If you can't be bothered to go through the process of straining the juice to make blackcurrant jelly, try this tasty jam. You have to boil the currants until they are tender before adding the sugar, but the jam, once made, has a lovely flavour and a chewy texture. There is loads of pectin in blackcurrants so, once the sugar is in, the jam will only need a few more minutes' cooking time.

Oh, and don't forget to wash the fruit well under cold running water – currants can be very dusty.

Put the currants and water in a large pan over a moderate heat. Once the mixture is boiling, cover the pan with a lid then simmer the fruit for about 30–40 minutes or until the berries are very soft.

Now stir in the sugar, turning the heat down until it has fully dissolved and there is no grittiness about the mixture. Turn the heat back up and bring to a full rolling boil. Test for a set after 2 minutes, then at 1-minute intervals until you have achieved a set (see page 166).

Pot into hot sterilized jars, and cover and label in the usual fashion (see page 166). Keeps for six to twelve months.

I love making marmalade, and buy quantities of Seville oranges as soon as I see them in the shops. I find the warmth of the kitchen, the heady smell of citrus and the brilliant colour of the marmalade a perfect antidote to cold January days.

There are two stages to making marmalade. The first is cooking the fruit, and the second boiling for a set. This may sound complicated but is quite straightforward. The pre-cooking is necessary, as the peel of citrus fruit becomes hard if the sugar is added before the peel has been thoroughly cooked. Once this happens there is no going back, and you will have very chewy marmalade.

I always cook my fruit whole, finding the whole process of removing the pips and cutting the peel so much easier when the fruit is soft. Use only fresh good-quality fruit. Wash all fruit well in hot water, scrubbing waxed fruit with a scourer.

The following is a good basic recipe which you can adapt to suit your taste. I add extra goodies sometimes: chopped crystallized ginger, a good slug of whisky or even some chopped red chillies. Each gives a bit of zip to the breakfast table.

Orange Marmalade

Fills 7 medium (300ml/10fl oz) jars

1.25kg/2¾lb Seville oranges
2.25 litres/4 pints/8 cups water, to begin with
1.5kg/3lb 5oz/8¼ cups unrefined granulated white sugar

Wash the oranges under warm running water then place them, whole, along with the measured water, in your chosen large pan. Bring the mixture to the boil. Cover with a lid and simmer for about 40–50 minutes or until the fruit is very soft.

Using a slotted spoon, remove the fruit from the pan. Measure the liquid remaining in the pan and, if necessary, make this up to 1.3 litres/2¼ pints by adding cold water. Add the sugar to the pan and let it begin to dissolve off the heat.

Cut the cooked oranges in half, and scrape all the seeds and pith into a bowl.

Finely shred the peel and return it to the pan. Scoop the reserved pith and seeds into a square of muslin. Tie this firmly and place this in the pan also.

Simmer to dissolve the sugar completely, stirring, then bring the mixture up to the boil. Simmer for 10 minutes. Continue to cook until a set is achieved (see page 166) – about 5–25 minutes, depending on the amount of marmalade in the pan, the size of the pan, etc. Remove the bag of pith and pips and squeeze to extract as much juice as possible. Discard the contents of the muslin.

Pot the marmalade in the usual manner (see page 166). It keeps for twelve months.

Lemon Curd

Fills 2 small (150ml/5fl oz) jars

5 eggs, beaten
200g/7oz/1 cup caster (superfine) sugar
175ml/6fl oz/¾ cup double (heavy) cream
finely grated zest and juice of 3 lemons

This unconventional recipe for lemon curd uses cream in place of the more usual butter. The result is a little lighter, and I've found no difference in the keeping qualities.

Combine all the ingredients together then pour into a shallow frying pan and place over a low heat.

Stir the mixture, over heat, until the curd thickens. All the warnings about not letting the mixture boil are important here. If you overheat the curd it will separate, and you will have sweet scrambled egg.

Patience is called for, as you may have to cook for about 15–20 minutes before the mixture coats the back of your spoon. You are looking for something about as thick as home-made mayonnaise.

Pot into hot sterilized jars and cover with a lid in the usual fashion (see page 166). Store in the fridge for up to three months.

Lime, grapefruit and even orange can also be made into curd. I always add some lemon juice to these other citrus to ensure the flavour is acidic enough.

Redcurrant Curd

Fills 4 small (150ml/5fl oz) jars

400g/14oz/2½ cups redcurrants
115g/4oz/1 stick unsalted butter
200g/7oz/1 cup caster (superfine) sugar
5 large eggs

Whilst I love the purity of lemon curd, I also make curd with all those tart summer berries – raspberries, black-currants, gooseberries and redcurrants. The method I'm using here I encountered when visiting the United States and, though rather unusual, it works well.

I am very impatient so always make my curds in a large open pan over a low heat. Provided you never leave the pan, and watch it like a hawk, the curd will be fine. The faint-hearted should use a double boiler.

Wash the currants under running water to remove any grit or dust. Place them in a pan over a low heat with just the water that clings to them then cook until the fruit softens and boils, about 20 minutes.

Rub the mixture through a sieve into a bowl. Now place the butter, sugar and eggs in the bowl of a food processor and whiz until well mixed.

Tip this, plus the contents of the bowl into which you sieved the fruit, into a wide shallow pan and place over a low heat. Stirring constantly, heat the mixture until it becomes smooth. Now lower the heat even more, and again stirring constantly, cook the curd until it thickens. This will take about 10 minutes. If at any time you feel the pan is too hot, lift it from the heat and stir vigorously.

When the mixture has reached the desired consistency – the curd will thicken more as it cools so you are looking for a consistency similar to thick pouring cream – pot it into hot sterilized jars (see page 165). Seal and label in the usual way (see page 166). Store in the refrigerator, where it will keep for six weeks.

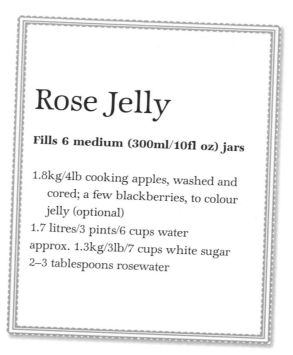

Rose Jelly

Fills 6 medium (300ml/10fl oz) jars

1.8kg/4lb cooking apples, washed and
     cored; a few blackberries, to colour
     jelly (optional)
1.7 litres/3 pints/6 cups water
approx. 1.3kg/3lb/7 cups white sugar
2–3 tablespoons rosewater

*Rosemary, thyme and other herb jellies
(such as lavender) can be made by cooking
the appropriate herbs – leaves and/or
flowers – with the apples and continuing
as below. Omit the rosewater.*

Roughly chop the apples and place them
and the blackberries (if using) in a large
pan. Add the water and simmer until the
apples are very soft – about 40 minutes.

Transfer the pulp into a jelly bag placed
over a glass bowl, and allow the mixture to
drip for several hours (overnight is best).
Don't be tempted to squeeze the bag, as the
jelly will be clouded if you do.

Measure the resulting liquid and allow
450g/1lb/2⅓ cups sugar to each 600ml/
1 pint/2 cups of liquid.

Pour the measured juice into a large,
heavy-based pan and bring slowly to the
boil. Lower the heat and add the sugar,
stirring until the sugar has dissolved.
Bring back to the boil and cook at a full
rolling boil until setting point is reached
(see page 166), about 5 minutes.

Skim off any scum that has appeared,
using a slotted spoon, and then add the
rosewater. Pot into hot sterilized jars and
cover in the usual fashion (see page 166).
Keeps for six to nine months.

✳ ✳

Vanilla-scented Prunes in Brandy

Fills 3 medium (300ml/10fl oz) jars

fresh tea made with 1 teaspoon Earl Grey
    or other tea leaves and 1 litre/2 pints/4¼ cups
    boiling water
1kg/2¼lb/6¾ cups no-soak or ready-to-eat prunes
1 whole vanilla pod (bean)
9 tablespoons light raw muscovado sugar
600ml/1 pint/2 cups brandy, plus extra if required

Prunes can be bottled at any time of year and are best kept for about six months before use. I spoon them and the brandy over ice-cream, put individual prunes in the base of sweet soufflés, or use them to stuff baked apples. They make fabulous presents for friends.

If you are in France you may find 'mi-cuit' prunes at the local market. These are very soft as they have only been lightly cooked and so will need no further soaking. More often I use those labelled either 'no-soak' or 'ready-to-eat'.

Make the tea using the tea leaves of your choice. Strain the brewed tea into a bowl and add the prunes, ensuring that they are all covered. Leave to soak overnight. This step is necessary even if you are using ready-to-eat prunes, as they will absorb the brandy more quickly if they are slightly rehydrated. The next day, have ready 3 medium sterilized jars (see page 165).

Drain the prunes well, patting them dry with kitchen paper (paper towels). Split open the vanilla pod (bean) and scrape out the seeds. Cut the pod into three pieces and reserve these.

Pack the prunes into the jars, adding 3 tablespoons of sugar to each jar and pouring in sufficient brandy to cover the fruits. Now divide the vanilla seeds between the jars along with a piece of the pod as well.

Seal the jars and give them a gentle shake, which will help the sugar dissolve, and mix in the vanilla seeds. Label, adding the date. Store the prunes in a cool dark pantry, shaking the jars gently about once a week or whenever you remember. The prunes will be ready to use in three to four months.

Spicy Orange & Cranberry Mincemeat

Fills 6 small (150ml/5fl oz) jars

100g/3½oz/½ cup dried cranberries
300g/10½oz/2 cups raisins
200g/7oz/1⅓ cups sultanas (golden raisins)
100g/3½oz/½ cup currants
100g/3½oz/½ cup glacé (candied) cherries
200g/7oz/1½ cups whole mixed candied peel, finely chopped
1 medium cooking apple, cored, peeled and grated
300g/10½oz/1½ cups soft brown sugar
55g/2oz/⅓ cup flaked almonds
finely grated zest and juice of 2 oranges
½ teaspoon ground cinnamon
3 teaspoons ground mixed spice
½ teaspoon freshly grated nutmeg
200g/7oz/1¾ sticks butter, melted
6 tablespoons brandy, or other alcohol of choice

This home-made mincemeat uses butter in place of beef suet, as I prefer the lighter flavour. Suet does theoretically give a slightly longer shelf life, though I have never had any problems.

When choosing your fruit, buy the best you can find. Mincemeat is a treat, a luxury preserve, so big juicy raisins and plump currants are called for. I prefer un-dyed cherries but it must be said that the bright red colour of dyed cherries does add a festive note. There is, though, one point at which you can make economies – use whatever brandy, whisky or liqueur you have lingering at the back of the cupboard. And, as ever, freshly ground spices make for a tastier mix.

Place all the dried fruit on a chopping board and roughly chop it using a large knife. If you have a food processor, pile the fruit into the bowl fitted with the metal blade and press the pulse button for a few seconds. You want the fruit to still be recognizable.

Now tip the chopped fruit into a large bowl and add all the remaining ingredients, except for the butter and whichever alcohol you have chosen. Mix well to start the sugar dissolving, then cover the bowl and leave in a cold place for 12–24 hours. Preheat the oven to 140°C/280°F/Gas Mark 1.

Melt the butter. Spread the mincemeat in an ovenproof dish and pour over the melted butter. Stir well, cover with foil and bake in the preheated oven for 2 hours.

Take the dish from the oven and allow to cool completely, stirring from time to time to mix everything together. Once the mince-meat is cold, stir in the brandy and pot into your sterilized jars. Cover and label; store in a cold dark larder for up to 3 months.

Spiced Pears in Red Wine

Fills 2 large (500ml/18fl oz) jars

1 bottle red wine
100g/3½oz/scant ⅓ cup clear honey
450g/1lb/2⅓ cups white sugar
4 x 7.5cm/3in cinnamon sticks
4 cloves
3cm/1¼in fresh root ginger, peeled and finely sliced
finely grated zest and juice of 2 lemons and 2 oranges
12–14 firm, ripe dessert pears, peeled, with stalks
brandy or vodka, to cover (see method)

You need to use small pears for this recipe, as that way you will fit more into each jar. I like Conference, but any just-ripe pears will be fine. I'm not too fussed about which wine you use, as the spices and honey will be the dominant flavours.

In a large preserving pan, combine the wine, honey, sugar, cinnamon sticks, cloves, sliced ginger, lemon and orange zest and juice. Bring the syrup to the boil and simmer for 5 minutes, stirring until the sugar has dissolved.

Add the pears and poach over a very low heat for 10–15 minutes or until just cooked through. Remove from the heat, carefully remove the pears, and pack into hot, sterilized jars (see page 165). Add some spices to each jar.

Return the pan to the heat and boil the cooking liquid over a high heat for 20–30 minutes until you have a thickish syrup. Divide the syrup between the jars, topping up with brandy or, for a cleaner flavour, vodka, to ensure that the pears are covered by the syrup.

Seal and label in the usual way (see page 166), and store in a cool, dark place for a month before use.

Spiced Roasted Plums

Fills 3 medium (300ml/10fl oz) jars

750g/1lb 10oz firm plums
300g/10½oz/1½ cups caster (superfine)
   sugar
400ml/14fl oz/1¾ cups red wine vinegar
10cm/4in cinnamon stick
a strip of orange zest
1–2 blades of mace
1 fresh red chilli, quartered

You'll need to use a firm plum for this recipe, so not Victorias. (Whilst they are my favourite eating plum, they contain far too much juice for pickling in this fashion.) I used Marjorie's Seedling but other firm ripe plums would be fine. Roasting the plums drives off even more juice and concentrates the flavours.

As I have said before, the joy of cooking for yourself is that you choose what goes in each dish, and with pickles the same rules apply. I like the taste of allspice with these plums, which makes them, to my mind, perfectly complement roast goose. You might prefer crushed coriander or cardamom.

Preheat the oven to 200°C/400°F/Gas Mark 6.

Begin by quartering and stoning your plums and placing the pieces on a baking sheet lined with non-stick paper. Sprinkle about 55g/2oz/¼ cup of the sugar over the plums and roast them in the preheated oven for 30 minutes.

Meanwhile prepare the spiced vinegar. Mix the remaining sugar with the vinegar in a stainless-steel saucepan and add the flavourings. Place over a low heat, stirring until the sugar dissolves, then bring to a boil and simmer for 5 minutes. Turn off and allow the flavours to infuse for a while.

Divide the plums between the sterilized jars (see page 165), pressing them down well with the back of a metal spoon so they are well packed in. Pour over the vinegar, tucking the spices and chilli into the jars. Cover and store for a month before using.

I like to make my own mixed spice for its wonderful intense flavour. I use it around Christmas time for puddings, pies, cakes and mincemeat.

Grind all together in a coffee grinder. Store it in a screw-top jar in a dark cupboard. Although best used within six weeks, this spice will keep for many months.

This is my spice mix,
but why not invent your own?
Black pepper, anise, mace
might all be to your taste.

Mixed Spice

Fills 1 spice jar

3 tablespoons coriander seeds
1 cinnamon stick
8 whole cloves
8 allspice berries
3 teaspoons freshly grated nutmeg
2 teaspoons ground ginger

PICKLES AND CHUTNEYS

Introduction

Making Chutneys, Pickles and Relishes

Just imagine walking into your larder, looking along the packed shelves and trying to choose between green tomato chutney, summer vegetable relish and sweet and sour pickled figs. A pipe dream? No, for whilst you and I may not have the perfect larder, we can easily make perfect pickles, chutneys and relishes.

Chutneys and pickles can be made from a wonderful variety of fruit and vegetables; you are limited only by your imagination, and what can be found at your farmers' market or grown in your garden. While I usually see what's about, then plan my pickles, it might be a good move to plan growing some of the more unusual vegetables for pickling. Shallots, especially, can be quite costly to buy in quantity, but they seem quite simple to grow. I say this as even I, who has no hint of a green thumb, can grow shallots. Yellow tomatoes would make an unusual ketchup, and why not grow a variety of peppers to add to your pickles or store bottled in vinegar ready for spicing your dishes through the year?

The traditional preserving agents here are vinegar and sugar which, with salt, allow for a long shelf life. Spices have a preserving effect, too, with chilli being a powerful preservative.

The distinction between chutneys and pickles is that chutneys are boiled until cooked and very thick, and they also tend to contain a relatively high sugar content. Pickles tend first to be brined to eliminate some of the water in the vegetables then they are either potted and covered with cold vinegar or cooked very briefly and covered with the hot vinegar. There is a third member of this team that is commonly called a relish. Relishes veer more towards chutneys than pickles and, often raw or only lightly cooked, they do not usually have the keeping qualities of chutneys. I do think the word 'relish' a delight, so my summer vegetable relish is really a chutney, but sounded so much more tasty when called a relish...

Chutney, Pickle and Relish Ingredients

As always when you are preserving something, it has to warrant the effort you put in, so always choose the freshest and best. I guess my only codicil to this would be that I have made chutneys from slightly bruised apples when properly prepared. I would urge caution if you feel chutney- and pickle-making is a way of avoiding waste when you have glut of vegetables in the garden. Whilst a bounteous crop of tomatoes can be turned into an excellent range of pickles, chutneys and ketchups, a glut of overgrown watery courgettes (zucchini) made into chutney may well sit on the larder shelf for months.

Small crisp vegetables are essential for pickles. These vegetables will need brining to remove much of the water naturally found in them. I also like to choose good-looking vegetables to give a bright fresh look to the pickles.

For chutneys you may use larger vegetables, ones that are full in flavour. They will be thoroughly cooked and so any excess liquid will be driven off as the chutney boils.

Salt and Brine

In almost every recipe for pickles, the vegetables or fruits will need brining or dry-salting before bottling. I find simple table salt works well. While I can't believe it matters desperately, there is traditional advice about when to brine and when to dry-salt. The more watery vegetables are dry-salted, so cucumbers, courgettes, aubergines, etc., are sprinkled with salt, directly on to the cut vegetables, then left overnight before being rinsed and dried on a tea towel (dish towel). The dryer vegetables – onions, cabbage and cauliflower, for instance – are usually brined, left in a salty bath, again for 24 hours, rinsed and dried as above. The object of both treatments is to remove as much of the naturally occurring water from the vegetables as possible. If you miss out this salting process, the water in the vegetables will leach into the vinegar, diluting it. If this happens and the acidity drops below the magic 6% (see below), the pickles will rot and spoil.

Vinegar

Vinegars vary widely in flavour and colour. It is said you can tell a nation's main beverage by the type of vinegar they use. Here in Britain we use malt vinegar derived from the brewing industry, whilst France uses wine vinegar and Spain sherry vinegar. I'm not sure this still holds, but it is a thought.

The essential thing to know here is that, when making pickles, you need a vinegar that has at least 6% acidity. This makes the vinegar strong enough to allow for adequate preservation. Apart from considering acidity, the flavour choice is yours.

When making highly flavoured chutneys, I often use distilled malt vinegar rather than the more costly wine vinegars. Cider vinegar is an excellent choice, too, but wine and even rice wine vinegars can be used. As the cooking process is part of the preserving, so vinegars of 5% acidity are perfectly acceptable here.

Sugar

Sugar is an essential part of chutney- and relish-making, and a desirable part of pickling. Sugar acts as a preserving agent alongside the vinegar and salt. It adds flavour and balances out acidity.

For clear pickles I lean towards using white sugar – granulated works well and is economical.

When making chutney, I find unrefined sugars work a treat as they add an extra layer of flavour. Light brown sugars are best, as dark or molasses sugar makes the finished relish have rather too deep a colour. Fresher-tasting relishes are better made with white or light unrefined sugars.

Spices

I have a passion for spice. For while I do love good plain flavours, it would be a dreadful shame not to use all those wonderful tastes and aromas that careful spicing adds to foods. Chutneys and pickles are no exception. As always, I urge you to use freshly ground spices, which have so much more taste than those bought ready ground.

In my recipes I have chosen the spices that I think work well, but you can make your own choices. The joy of cooking for yourself is that if you loathe cloves, as I do, they need never darken your kitchen door. Simply use a spice you like, and avoid one you don't like...

Some spices that are good in pickles and chutneys are: coriander, cumin, mustard seed, celery seed, cardamom, star anise, nutmeg, cinnamon, allspice, juniper, ginger, turmeric and, if you must, clove. Ginger I usually use either fresh or powdered, and turmeric, although available fresh from Asian markets, I use in its powdered form.

Equipment

A deep, wide enamelled pan is best for boiling chutneys. Any large stainless-steel or enamel saucepan will be fine for preparing vinegar for pickles. You may also need a metal spoon and jam funnel for filling the jars.

Any spotlessly clean glass jars are suitable for chutneys and pickles, but I find it best to use ones that come with vinegar-proof lids. These are easily identified by looking for a white plastic ring on the underside of the lid. Alternatively, glass jars with wired glass lids and rubber seals not only work well but also look very professional. See page 165 for how to sterilize your jars before filling.

Pickles

When making pickles, try to use the vegetables as soon as possible after harvesting. That is the time their natural sugars and flavours are at their most intense. Many differing combinations of vegetables can be used, so if you have small quantities, think about making a mixed pickle. Tucking a few chillies down the sides of clear pickles will look attractive and add spice.

A standard brine recipe is simple: the proportions are 225g/8oz/1 cup salt dissolved in 1.5 litres/2¾ pints/5½ cups water. The salt is dissolved in 300ml/10fl oz/1¼ cups boiling water first, then the remaining water is added cold to make up the volume. Brine is always used cold.

To brine vegetables, prepare your chosen vegetables, washing or peeling as necessary, and then cut to size. I find 1cm/½in best, but the choice is yours. Make your brine as above and allow to cool completely. Pour this into a large glass or china bowl and add the vegetables. Give them a stir, cover the bowl with clingfilm (plastic wrap), then put aside for 12–24 hours.

When you are ready to continue, drain the vegetables well, wash under cold running water then spread them on a couple of clean tea towels (dish towels) and pat them dry.

The next stage is to pack your vegetables into sterilized jars and pour over the spiced vinegar. Often this is added hot, but for very crisp pickles, i.e. onions and red cabbage, the vinegar is allowed to cool first. Using a metal spoon, press the vegetables down well into the jar and top up with vinegar.

Simple Spiced Vinegar for Pickling

1 litre/1¾ pints/3½ cups vinegar of 6% acidity
2 tablespoons light muscovado sugar
2–3 blades of mace
12 allspice berries
1 teaspoon black peppercorns
10cm/4in cinnamon stick, broken into small pieces
1–2 dried red chillies
1–2 dried bay leaves

Spiced vinegar is a handy ingredient to keep in the store cupboard. It can be used in cooking, as well as for pickling. If you have the time, you can simply tip the spices into the bottles of vinegar and leave to steep for 1–2 weeks. The spices will keep adding flavour, if left, for many months.

Place all the ingredients in a steel or enamelled saucepan and bring slowly up to boiling point. Take from the heat and allow to cool before use.

Potting Pickles

Prepare and brine your vegetables as above. For the best results, cabbage should be shredded, and onions, apart from pickling onions, quartered.

Pack the dry vegetables into spotlessly clean glass jars and cover with spiced vinegar, spooning a few of the whole spices into each jar. The vinegar should cover the vegetables by at least 1cm/½in.

Screw the lids on firmly and place in a cool dark larder for at least one month before using.

By following these easy steps you can create your own variations of pickles.

Chutneys

Sugar and vinegar provide the preserving elements, and long slow boiling both cooks the ingredients and reduces the mixture to a good mounding consistency.

Begin by picking your fruit and vegetables. You can use slightly over-ripe, and even some less than perfect specimens for chutney as long as you cut out any bruised and damaged parts.

Chop the vegetables to an even size. I find 1cm/½in cubes to be about right. Larger dried fruit such as dates, peaches and apricots are best chopped before use. Finely grate ginger and garlic. Always grind dry spices just before you need them, when they will then be at their most potent.

Cooking Chutney

Usually all the ingredients are placed in the pan together and this is put over a low heat. The mixture is then stirred often to ensure the sugar dissolves.

Once this has happened the heat is turned to moderate and the chutney is simmered until it is thick. This can often take an hour or more. It is important to stir the chutney from time to time, more often towards the end of cooking, when the chutney can catch on the base of the pan. Chutneys have a terrible tendency to stick and burn at the latter stage of cooking. I know to my cost how quickly this can happen, so the rule is never to leave the kitchen when you are cooking preserves.

To test if the chutney is done, drag a wooden spoon through the mixture on the bottom of the pan. The spoon should leave a clear channel with perhaps a little liquid seeping back. If the chutney flows back to cover the channel, boil for a little longer.

Potting Chutney

Have ready hot, sterilized jars (see page 165) and vinegar-proof lids.

Place the jars on a tray or baking sheet near the preserving pan. Using a jam funnel, spoon the hot chutney into the jars, leaving about 1.5cm/⅝in head space. If the chutney is very thick or chunky, it is sometimes necessary to use a spoon to pack the mixture down into the jars to avoid air gaps. I use a clean metal teaspoon to do this.

Once the jar is filled, screw on the lids. You may need to tighten these when the jars have cooled. Do label jars carefully.

Storing Chutneys and Pickles

Chutneys and pickles are best stored in a cold dark pantry. All chutneys and pickles need a period of maturation for the flavours to develop and for the harsh vinegary tang to soften. Mostly, I try to keep my chutneys and pickles for six weeks before using. They keep for several years, but over time the chutneys will darken and the pickles become soft, so ideally use them within the year.

Green Tomato Chutney

Fills 4 medium (300ml/10fl oz) jars

600g/1lb 5oz/4½ cups green tomatoes, roughly
  chopped
350g/12oz/1¼ cups onions, peeled and roughly
  chopped
4 plump garlic cloves
1–2 hot red chillies
½ teaspoon each of fennel seeds and celery seeds
200g/7oz/1 cup soft brown sugar
300ml/10fl oz/1¼ cups cider or wine vinegar
1 dessertspoon salt
55g/2oz tamarind paste (optional)

*At the end of summer, I always seem
to have a crop of recalcitrant tomatoes
which simply refuse to ripen. In the past,
I have left them on the vines, hoping that
the late autumn sun will work wonders,
but they simply wither and perish. So
now I make this chutney. The tamarind
is optional; I had some in the cupboard
and liked its sour taste. Serve with
the usual suspects: cheese, cold meats
and pâtés.*

Blitz the tomatoes and onions in a food
processor until roughly medium chopped.
You don't want a purée, but again the
pieces don't want to be too big.

Peel and crush the garlic. Chop the
chillies, first removing the seeds if you
want a milder heat. Crush the fennel and
celery seeds together in a pestle and mortar
until quite fine.

Place everything into a large saucepan
and, stirring from time to time, bring to
the boil. Turn the heat down to a simmer
and cook the chutney until it is thick,
stirring whenever you pass the pan. This
will take about 20–30 minutes, depending
on how juicy your tomatoes were.

Pot into clean sterilized jars, top with
vinegar-proof lids and seal (see page 166).
Label and store in a cool dark place for six
to nine months.

Mango & Lemon Chutney

Fills 6 medium (300ml/10fl oz) jars

675g/1½lb/4½ cups mixed dried fruit (dates, apricots,
    figs, peaches, raisins, etc.)
1.4kg/3lb 2oz mangoes
2 lemons, scrubbed
2 large onions, peeled and chopped
6 plump garlic cloves, peeled
55g/2oz/¼ cup fresh root ginger, peeled
2–4 fresh red chillies
seeds from 4–6 cardamom pods
1 teaspoon mustard seeds
675g/1½lb/3½ cups light muscovado sugar
1 tablespoon salt
1 litre/1¾ pints/3½ cups distilled vinegar

Using lemons and fresh chillies gives extra zip to this chutney. Add whatever combination of dried fruit suits your taste, but try to make it as varied as possible. This recipe takes very little time to cook, as the high proportion of dried fruit helps it thicken quickly. The chutney is excellent with curries and with cold meat. It also makes a good sauce for cold chicken if mixed one-third chutney, two-thirds mayonnaise.

Cut the dried fruit into even-sized pieces – about 1cm/½in. Peel the mangoes, then cut the flesh from the large stone and chop.

Place the lemons, onions, garlic, ginger and chillies in a blender or processor and whiz until finely chopped. Grind the spices – in a mortar or spice grinder – until fine.

Mix all the ingredients in a large heavy-bottomed pan and bring to the boil. Turn down the heat and simmer until the mixture is thick – about 30 minutes.

Pot into clean sterilized jars, top with vinegar-proof lids and seal (see page 166). Label and store in a cool dark place for six to nine months.

Summer Vegetable Relish

Fills 4 medium (300ml/10fl oz) jars

1kg/2¼lb tomatoes
600g/1lb 5oz aubergines
800g/1¾lb courgettes (zucchini) (small are best)
400/14oz red peppers
1 whole garlic bulb
3 red onions
2 hot fresh chillies, or to taste
2 tablespoons salt
1 tablespoon each of fennel seeds and coriander seeds
2 tablespoons dried oregano
650g/1lb 7oz/4 cups white sugar
1 litre/1¾ pints/3½ cups cider vinegar

This lovely relish will bring a taste of summer to even the darkest winter's day. It's a mix of all those vegetables you have gluts of – a kind of ratatouille chutney!

Prepare all the vegetables. Chop the tomatoes, cutting away any hard cores. Trim and dice the aubergines and courgettes (zucchini). Seed and dice the peppers. Peel and chop the garlic and onions. Chop the chillies.

Mix the salt, seeds and oregano in your mortar and crush together with the pestle.

Now mix everything in your largest pan and place over a moderate heat.

Stir often until the mixture has begun to boil. Turn down the heat and simmer, stirring regularly, until the relish has reduced by about half and is thick – about 30–40 minutes.

Pot into clean sterilized jars, top with vinegar-proof lids and seal (see page 165). Label and store in a cool dark place. Store for two to three months before using.

Sweet Mustard Pickles

**Fills 1 large (500ml/18fl oz) or
2 medium (300ml/10fl oz) jars**

2 large or 4–6 small cucumbers
1 red pepper
1 large red onion
1–2 fresh green chillies, or to taste
55g/2oz/¼ cup salt
1 teaspoon each of fennel and celery
    seeds
1 teaspoon dry mustard powder
1 teaspoon dried dill
500ml/18fl oz/2¼ cups distilled vinegar
150g/5½oz/scant 1¼ cups white sugar

*I love these cucumber pickles, partly for the
taste, but also for the ease of making, and
the fact that they are ready to eat within
a couple of days.*

*Store them in the fridge and enjoy them
with cheese on toast, burgers and cold
meats – pretty much anything...*

If you are using large cucumbers cut them
in half lengthways and, using a teaspoon,
scoop out the seeds. Cut the cucumbers into
fine slices. Take the seeds from the pepper
and cut the flesh into fine slices. Peel, halve
and finely slice the onion. Slice the chilli.

Arrange the vegetables in a shallow
bowl and scatter on the salt. Leave
overnight. The following morning, drain
and wash the vegetables, spreading them
on clean tea towels (dish towels) to drain
and dry.

In a pestle and mortar, crush the fennel
and celery seeds, along with the mustard
and dried dill. Have ready your hot
sterilized jars (see page 165).

In a large saucepan mix the vinegar,
sugar and crushed spices. Bring this
mixture to the boil and simmer for
5 minutes. Add the vegetables and cook
at a full boil for 1 minute only. Remove the
vegetables with a slotted spoon and pack
them into the sterilized jars. Pour over the
hot pickling liquid and seal and label.

Store in a cold dark place for up to three
months. Once opened, store the pickles in
the fridge.

Always use a clean spoon to serve
pickles, it's easy to contaminate
the jar if you double-dip with
your fork!

Instant Marinated Olives

Makes 400g/14oz

400g/14oz mixed olives in brine (drained
   weight)
2 teaspoons dried mixed herbs
2 dried red chillies, crushed
1 large garlic clove, peeled and crushed
about 4 tablespoons olive oil
½ lemon or lime, finely sliced
a few pieces of finely cut orange zest

*Marinating tinned olives transforms the
flavour. These olives can be eaten about
2 hours after marinating and will keep
for several days.*

Drain the olives from the brine and place
in a large bowl. Add the herbs, chillies and
garlic and enough oil to coat everything.
Mix in the lemon slices and orange zest,
cover with clingfilm (plastic wrap), and
allow the olives to sit for about 1–2 hours
before use.

   They will keep for up to three weeks
in the fridge.

Serve these olives as part of an
ante pasta plate, alongside finely
sliced meats, mozzarella and some
sun-dried tomatoes

Cauliflower & Onion Pickles

**Fills approx. 3 medium
(300ml/10fl oz) jars**

500g/18oz small onions
1 large cauliflower

Brine
225g/8oz/1 cup table salt
1.5 litres/2¾ pints/5½ cups water

Sauce
25g/1oz/¼ cup plain (all-purpose) flour
55g/2oz/½ cup dry mustard powder
225g/8oz/scant 1¼ cups light muscovado
   sugar
750ml/26fl oz/3¼ cups distilled malt
   vinegar
1 teaspoon each of coriander and cumin
   seeds, crushed
1 tablespoon turmeric

*I guess this is a version of piccalilli, but
without the bits I don't like! It's quite
simple to make, and delicious served with
almost any cold meat. It is essential when
serving pork pie, and is even good with
strong British cheese, like Cheddar.*

Make the brine by dissolving the salt in
300ml/10fl oz/1¼ cups hot water then
making up to the stated volume with
cold water.

Prepare the vegetables. Peel the onions,
cutting them into quarters if large. Cut the
cauliflower into small florets. Place these in
a large china or glass bowl and pour over
the cooled brine. Cover and leave overnight.

The next day, or after 12 hours, drain
the vegetables well, then wash under
running cold water. Spread over a clean tea
towel (dish towel) and pat dry.

Make the sauce. Mix the flour, mustard
and sugar together and make into a paste
with some of the vinegar. Scrape the
mixture into a large steel saucepan and
add the remaining ingredients.

Cook over a medium heat, whisking
constantly until the mixture thickens and
boils. Simmer, whisking, for 2–3 minutes
to cook the flour. Now add the dried
vegetables and cook for 3 minutes.

Using a slotted spoon, divide the
vegetables between hot sterilized jars
(see page 165) and then top up with sauce.
If the sauce doesn't cover the vegetables,
simply pour in a little extra vinegar.
Screw on vinegar-proof lids and store for
at least two weeks before using. Keeps
for three months.

Sweet & Sour Chillied Figs

Fills 2 medium (300ml/10fl oz) jars

500g/1lb 2oz/3¼ cups dried figs, stems
  removed, finely sliced
85g/3oz/½ cup dark muscovado sugar
2–3 dried chillies, finely chopped
300ml/10fl oz/1¼ cups red wine vinegar,
  plus extra if necessary

Always pick the best-quality dried fruit just as you would if you were buying fresh. Dried figs are often coated in cornflour (cornstarch) so if your figs look dusty and white, wash them well and allow them to drain before continuing with the recipe.

I always serve these preserves with pâtés, but they also work well with cheese and meat pies.

Put the figs in a pan with the sugar, chillies and vinegar and warm gently, stirring until the sugar dissolves. Simmer the mixture gently for 3–5 minutes until the figs begin to soften. If the mixture is very dry, add more vinegar.

Allow the pickle to cool a little before potting into hot, sterilized jars, covering with vinegar-proof seals, and labelling (see page 166). Allow the figs to mature for about four weeks before using them. Store them in a cold dark cupboard or larder, where they will keep for up to a year.

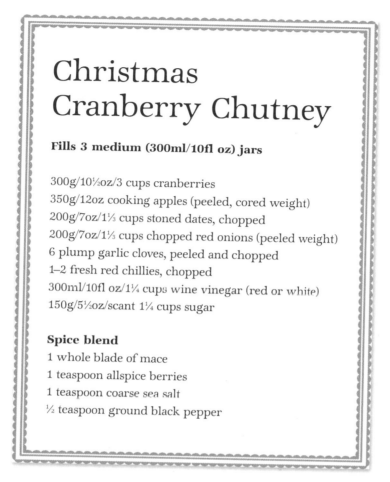

Christmas Cranberry Chutney

Fills 3 medium (300ml/10fl oz) jars

300g/10½oz/3 cups cranberries
350g/12oz cooking apples (peeled, cored weight)
200g/7oz/1⅓ cups stoned dates, chopped
200g/7oz/1⅓ cups chopped red onions (peeled weight)
6 plump garlic cloves, peeled and chopped
1–2 fresh red chillies, chopped
300ml/10fl oz/1¼ cups wine vinegar (red or white)
150g/5½oz/scant 1¼ cups sugar

Spice blend
1 whole blade of mace
1 teaspoon allspice berries
1 teaspoon coarse sea salt
½ teaspoon ground black pepper

Whilst you don't have to save this chutney to eat at Christmas, its lovely deep red colour, fragrant spicing and rich taste make it the perfect relish to serve with leftover cold meats like turkey and ham.

I use white sugar for this to keep the colour bright, but light muscovado would also work well.

Begin by placing the fruits, onions, garlic and chillies in a large stainless-steel saucepan and adding the vinegar. Place on a medium heat and bring the mixture to the boil. Cover loosely with a lid and simmer until everything is very soft – about 40 minutes.

Using a pestle and mortar, crush the spices, salt and pepper together until finely ground.

Add these and the sugar to the pan and stir until the sugar has dissolved. Now, with the lid removed, continue to cook the chutney until thick – a further 30 minutes. Stir often and keep a close eye on the pot as, once the sugar is in the mixture, it has a tendency to stick and burn.

Pot into clean sterilized jars, top with vinegar-proof lids and seal (see page 166). Label and store in a cool dark place for six to nine months.

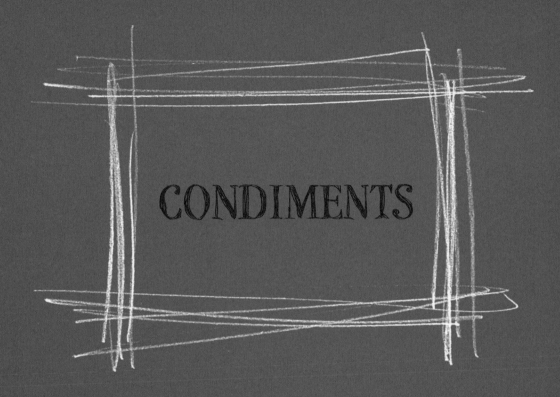

CONDIMENTS

Introduction

Condiments

Condiments, according to my dictionary, are substances such as salt and ketchup, that are added to food to give flavour. A rather bland definition seeing as we're talking intense flavours here, I feel. All of us are familiar with the trinity of table condiments – salt, pepper and mustard – but that is just a starting point when it comes to this subject.

There are wonderful tales to be told about table sauces like Tabasco and Worcestershire sauce, which seem to have in common inventors who found their sauces so unpalatable at first that both men forgot about them for several years. The chance rediscovery of bottles of sauce followed by the tasting found that, over the course of time, the sauces had developed wonderful flavours and their harsh vinegary tang had mellowed. Success, both culinary and financial, followed.

It is the age in these table sauces that adds such a lot to our meals. Age is more interesting than youth, and never was that saying more correct than in food. Mature cheese tastes more complex than fresh, salami more layered in flavour than fresh pork. It is the same with table sauces: the mix of fruits, salts and vinegars combine to add more than the sum of the parts, with just a drop of age thrown in.

Here are some of the most usual condiments.

Salt

This is a condiment so highly regarded that we have a host of sayings that involve salt: 'worth his salt', 'below the salt', 'take it with a grain of salt', 'salt of the earth' are but a few.

Salt was and still is an essential addition to food to enhance flavour. The addition of salt to food brings out its flavour, and even sweet foods have an affinity with salt; adding a pinch of salt to chocolate cake will make it taste more chocolatey.

Salt comes from two main sources: sea salt and rock salt. Sea salt is prepared by evaporation, often in salt pans where careful gathering of salt crystals from the increasingly concentrated saline in the pools, means that pure salt can be harvested and the other bitter minerals found in sea water are left behind. Some commonly available sea salts are Maldon, Cornish sea salt, Anglesey salt, *fleur de sel* and *sel gris de Guérande*.

Rock salt comes from seams of salt left when changes to topography isolated seas during and after the ice age. This salt is either quarried or dissolved in water, pumped to the surface and then the saline is evaporated to give powdered salt. Whilst much of this salt is made into fine table and kosher salt, there are high-end rock salts, the most readily available and expensive of which are Himalayan pink salt and Hawaiian lava black salt.

The source of the salt, how it is processed and the size of the crystals will give each salt a distinct flavour. Opinions vary as to which is the best salt. I have three sorts in my kitchen. I use simple fine table salt mainly in cooking – when boiling pasta and vegetables, for making brines and always in baking breads, cakes and biscuits.

I use kosher salt, a very pure coarse crystalline salt, for all my dry salting of fish, meat and vegetables. I find the fact that it dissolves slowly on the surface of the food gives a better result than the harsher effect of fine powdered salt.

Maldon salt, with its wonderfully fragile, enormous crystals is my idea of salt heaven. It has a clean flavour and I use it to season food and as a table salt. There is something wonderfully sensual about Maldon salt and how it feels when you crush it between your fingers. It adds a wonderfully salty hit when sprinkled on top of food before it goes in the oven, and looks fantastic on breads like foccacia and olive loaves.

Pepper

Peppercorns are the fruit of the flowering vine *Piper nigrum*. This grows in tropical and semi-tropical conditions, and is one of the world's most traded spices. It has a wonderful hot complex flavour that has been added to both sweet and savoury dishes for many thousand of years. It is mentioned in Egyptian papyri, in medieval Europe pepper formed the centre of the spice trade, and it was said to be worth its weight in gold. This isn't really surprising when you consider pepper had to travel overland from India. Consumption of huge quantities of spice in food in the late Middle Ages was not simply a ruse to cover tainted meat, it was the beginning of conspicuous consumption. Only the very wealthy could afford such amounts of such a rare spice...

Pepper grows mainly in India, Vietnam, Brazil and Malaya with Tellicherry, an Indian peppercorn, being one of the most fragrant.

Pepper is not only a savoury spice, it is found in mixed spice and is the main spice in my *panforte di Siena* (see page 100).

Black pepper is made from the berries harvested just before they fully ripen, which is when they are at their most pungent. They are boiled briefly then dried, either mechanically or in the sun, before being packed and shipped. White peppercorns are the centre of the fully ripe berry, so they have a somewhat milder flavour. Here the berries are soaked in water for several days to remove the outer fruit, and then the now white berries are dried and sold.

Green peppercorns are unripe berries picked before the black ones, then lightly processed and packed in brine to give a greener fresher flavour. While these peppercorns can be bought fresh from oriental markets, they do not keep well. Pink peppercorns are not pepper at all, but the berries of the Brazilian pepper tree, and are more correctly labelled 'Baie Rose'.

Pepper keeps well, but like all spices is best used freshly ground. If you use a lot of pepper, grind a couple of tablespoons in a spice mill and store in a screw-top jar where it will keep its intensity for a couple of weeks. I simply have several peppermills scattered around the kitchen and dining room.

Mustard

Mustard seed is the fruit of a member of the Brassica or cabbage family. Both white and yellow mustards are grown easily in Europe, while black mustard is mainly grown in Asia.

The yellow fields of mustard flowers in June formed part of the agricultural calendar in my Norfolk childhood, where quantities of mustard was grown for the Colman's factory in Norwich. Harvested in September, this mustard is milled, de-husked and then sold either as a powder or ready mixed.

Wholegrain mustards are a later addition to the mustard range and were first popular in France which, along with the UK and Germany, are the highest consumers of mustard in Europe. Wholegrain and flavoured mustards are very popular now and, whilst I've given one recipe on page 222, you will be able to create many more of your own.

Refined mustard, ground mustard that has had the husks removed, keeps well as a powder, but soon loses its pungency when mixed with water. I like to mix mustard for the table about 10 minutes before it's needed.

Mustard oil has a pungent flavour and, although commonly used in Indian cooking, I would suggest it should be used with caution. Italian *mostarda de frutta* is a condiment made by immersing candied fruits in a syrup laced with mustard oil. It is commonly served with that Italian celebration dish, *bollito misto*.

Ketchups and Table Sauces

Ketchup long pre-dates the time Henry John Heinz hit upon a recipe that was to bring wealth to the company and despair to mothers like me who might prefer their children to taste the food being offered as offered rather than covered in a rich sweet sauce!

Originally 'ketchup' was the name for any savoury sauce. The word might have come from Asia where kecap is the name of a spicy fish sauce. Indeed, recipes for anchovy ketchup date back to the late 1700s, when it was a much-needed addition to the table when served with plain boiled foods. Ketchups have since been made with any number of fruits and vegetables, including apricots, tomatoes and mushrooms.

They have in common a dense texture and a sharp, spicy flavour and can not only be used as a table sauce, but as an addition to many recipes.

Sauce Marie Rose, for instance, is a mixture of equal parts of tomato ketchup and mayonnaise, and the wonderfully named chicken ketchycola, a recipe from the deep South of the United States, is made from the ingredients named in the title!

Here in Britain, our favourite sauce is the rather drably named 'brown' sauce. This table sauce dates back to the 1800s, and has graced tables both high and low. I make my own, and love the rich complex flavour. Serve it with egg and chips – sublime. Another traditional British sauce is Cumberland sauce, a rather jammy condiment often served with lamb, though I also serve it with hot ham and roast game. But we are not at all xenophobic when it comes to sauces, and have taken barbecue sauce, hoisin sauce and chilli sauces to our hearts. Balsamic vinegar is a newcomer on the table, but flavoured vinegars, so simple to make, work well in seasoning so many dishes.

Sugar

Although we consider sugar to be a condiment more suited to the dessert table, some of our best-loved sauces are sweet, and illustrate well the importance of sugar in rounding out flavours and dampening down the heat from chillies.

❧❧❧

A range of condiments on the table allows each person to add an individual touch to their meal, customizing their dish to suit their taste. And that suits me.

Cumberland Sauce

Fills 2 medium (300ml/10fl oz) jars

3 oranges

3 lemons

500g/18oz/2⅓ cups redcurrant jelly
   (see page 178)

150ml/5fl oz/½ cup port

1 dessertspoon dry mustard powder

1 small onion, peeled and finely chopped

a pinch of ground mace

4 tablespoons cider vinegar

A useful sauce for all seasons. Although most often served with game, this redcurrant works wonderfully with Reform lamb cutlets, a favourite of mine served hot or cold.

Using a potato peeler, peel off the rind of the fruit, making sure all the pith is left behind. Cut the rind into thin strips. Have ready a pan of boiling water and drop the rind into this. Cook for 1 minute, then drain and repeat this step once more. Drain again and place the blanched rind on kitchen paper (paper towels) to cool.

Squeeze and strain the juice of 2 of the oranges and 2 of the lemons. In a medium pan, bring this to the boil with all the remaining ingredients, apart from the rind. Simmer for a further 15 minutes over a low heat, stirring to ensure that the jelly melts evenly and doesn't catch. Add the shredded rind and boil for a further 5–10 minutes until the sauce starts to thicken.

Pot into hot sterilized jars and top with lids (see pages 165–6). Cool and store in a cold, dark pantry. Keeps for two to three months.

Seriously Festive Cranberry Sauce

Fills 3–4 small (150ml/5fl oz) jars

1 medium clementine or satsuma
500g/18oz/scant 5¼ cups fresh or frozen
    cranberries
10cm/4in cinnamon stick
juice of 1 lemon
115g/4oz/generous ¾ cup caster
    (superfine) sugar
115g/4oz/1 cup shelled pecan nuts,
    chopped
125ml/4fl oz/½ cup ruby port

*This sauce has lots of goodies in as befits
a Christmas treat. Pot into small jars and
give it to friends as gifts when visiting.
So much better than socks.*

*A little extra port can be stirred in just
before serving.*

Cut the clementine or satsuma in half and
remove any pips plus any really stringy
pith. Now finely chop the fruit, flesh and
peel together.

Place this along with the cranberries,
cinnamon stick and the lemon juice in a
pan over a low heat. Cook until the berries
start to pop, then turn down the heat and
stir in the sugar. Stir often until the sugar
has dissolved. Now add the nuts and port
and bring to the boil. Cook over a high heat
for 3–5 minutes until thickened.

Pot into sterilized jars, label and cover
(see pages 165–6). Keeps for two to three
months in a cool larder.

You really should store this sauce for about two to three months before you use it, as the harsh flavour of the vinegar and spices softens, to give a wonderfully dense sauce that's quite sublime with egg and chips, and is essential with bacon sandwiches.

Wash and stone the plums and place in a large pan with the dates, raisins, onion, garlic, chillies, ginger, coriander, allspice, salt and 500ml/18fl oz/2¼ cups of the vinegar. Bring to the boil and simmer until the fruit is very soft – about 30–40 minutes.

Liquidize and sieve or put through a mouli and return to a clean pan with the remaining vinegar, the turmeric, sugar and nutmeg. Simmer for a further 30 minutes or until the sauce is thick.

Pour into sterilized bottles, seal and label (see pages 165–6), and store for at least a month before use. It will keep for twelve months.

Home-made Brown Sauce

Fills 6 medium (300ml/10fl oz) jars

1.8kg/4lb plums
175g/6oz/scant 1¼ cup stoned dates, roughly chopped
115g/4oz/¾ cup raisins
3 large onions, peeled and chopped
1 garlic bulb, cloves peeled and chopped
2–3 fresh hot red chillies, or to taste
1 teaspoon dried chilli flakes
55g/2oz/¼ cup fresh root ginger, peeled and finely chopped
1 tablespoon coriander seeds
1 teaspoon allspice berries
55g/2oz/¼ cup salt
750ml/26fl oz/3¼ cups cider vinegar
1 tablespoon ground turmeric
280g/10oz/2¼ cups granulated sugar
½ nutmeg, freshly grated

Roast Tomato Ketchup

Fills approx. 6 medium (300ml/10fl oz) jars

3kg/6½lb very ripe tomatoes
8 plump garlic cloves, peeled and roughly chopped
2 tablespoons olive oil
a little coarse sea salt and freshly ground black pepper
2–3 sprigs fresh thyme
500g/18oz/3⅓ cups onions, peeled and chopped
1 large red pepper, seeded and chopped
200g/7oz celery, trimmed and chopped
250ml/9fl oz/scant 1¼ cups cider vinegar
225g/8oz/scant 1¼ cups granulated sugar
a good slug of Tabasco sauce (optional)

Spice mix
12 cloves
about 15–20 allspice berries
1 teaspoon celery seeds
10cm (4in) cinnamon stick, broken into pieces
1 teaspoon black peppercorns
2 tablespoons salt

Preheat the oven to 200ºC/400ºF/Gas Mark 6.

Cut the tomatoes in half and lay the halves on a baking sheet. Scatter on the roughly chopped garlic and then drizzle over the oil, with a good pinch of sea salt and the thyme. Place in the preheated oven and roast for 20–30 minutes. The tomatoes should shrink in size and smell delicious.

Scrape the tomatoes, plus all the juices, herbs etc., into a large enamelled preserving pan. Add the chopped onion, pepper, celery and half the vinegar. Cover and cook gently over a moderate heat for approximately 15 minutes until all the ingredients are very soft. Pass the mixture through a fine sieve or mouli.

Place all the whole spices into a coffee or spice grinder and whiz until finely ground.

Return the tomato purée to the cleaned pan and add the sugar, remaining vinegar, and the ground spice mix. Simmer for about 15–20 minutes, stirring frequently, until the mixture thickens. Don't let the sauce catch on the bottom of the pan.

Remove from the heat, stir in some Tabasco if you like, then pot into hot sterilized jars or bottles, and seal with vinegar-proof lids (see pages 165–6). Remember to label clearly. Store in a cold dark room. This ketchup keeps for six months or more, but the longer you store, the less vibrant the colour.

Roasting the tomatoes gives a wonderfully sweet, sticky flavour to this ketchup. Whilst you might think making your own ketchup is a bit of a chore, I hope this recipe will change your mind. It really does taste wonderful, and what I love about serving this is I know exactly what goes into it: nothing artificial at all!

This is my favourite barbecue sauce, but as it's rather sticky and sweet it has a tendency to burn easily. Baste it on to the food towards the end of cooking. Also remember to tip the sauce into a bowl for basting to avoid cross contamination.

Place all the ingredients in a large saucepan and whisk together until smooth. Bring the mixture slowly to the boil, whisking occasionally, until the sugar is dissolved. Simmer for 10–15 minutes or until the mixture thickens and becomes syrupy.

Pour into hot sterilized bottles, seal with vinegar-proof lids, and label (see pages 165–6). Store in a cold pantry or the fridge for up to three months.

Smoky Barbecue Sauce

Fills 2 medium (300ml/10fl oz) jars

250ml/9fl oz/scant ¼ cup orange or apple juice
175g/6oz/¾ cup light muscovado sugar
200ml/7fl oz/¾ cup Worcestershire sauce
200ml/7fl oz/¾ cup dark soy sauce
150ml/5fl oz/scant ¾ cup cider vinegar
100ml/3½fl oz/½ cup tomato purée
50ml/2fl oz/¼ cup chilli sauce
4 garlic cloves, peeled and crushed
2 tablespoons mild ready-made mustard
Tabasco sauce, to taste

Do make sure all barbecued food is cooked through. Burgers and sausages are most vulnerable to bacteria, as they both contain minced meat.

Fruit and Herb Vinegars

These tasty vinegars are simple to make and enhance anyone's store-cupboard. You can use almost any summer fruit, though raspberries and blackberries seem to take the flavour well. You can *use frozen or fresh fruit, everything is done in minutes, and you will never have to eat a dull salad again. I most often use tarragon to flavour herb vinegars, but the choice is yours.*

Raspberry Vinegar

Makes 300ml/10fl oz

115g/4oz/¾ cup fresh or frozen
    raspberries
2–3 tablespoons caster (superfine) sugar
250ml/9fl oz/scant 1¼ cup white wine
    vinegar

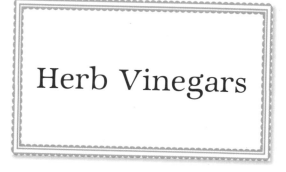

Herb Vinegars

These are even easier. Simply tuck sprigs of your favourite herbs into bottles of white wine or cider vinegar, and leave to infuse for a couple of weeks before using.

Mix the ingredients together, mashing the fruit into the vinegar. Put the mix into a jar and leave for 2–3 days, shaking the jar from time to time. You can add extra sugar if your tastes run to a sweeter flavour.

Don't be afraid to mix the herbs or even add a ripe chilli or two and a spoonful of sugar.

Honey Mustard

Fills 1 medium (300ml/10fl oz) jar

100g/3½oz/½ cup mustard seeds
about 250ml/9fl oz/scant 1¼ cups cider
  vinegar
4–6 tablespoons clear honey
1 teaspoon salt

Home-made mustard is delicious, and quite simple to make. I soak the seeds overnight to soften them, but you could bypass this step and use a coffee or spice mill to grind them before transferring the powder to a mixing bowl or food processor and adding the remaining ingredients.

Dried chilli flakes can be added for those mad enough to like even hotter mustard...

Put the seeds into a glass bowl and cover with vinegar, reserving the remaining vinegar. Cover with clingfilm (plastic wrap) and leave to marinate overnight.

Tip the contents of the bowl into a food processor and whiz until finely ground. You will need to add some of the remaining vinegar from time to time to ensure the paste does not become too thick.

Once the mustard is a texture you like, add honey to taste, but no less than 4 tablespoons, and stir in the salt.

Mix thoroughly then pot and cover in a sterilized jar (see page 165). Keeps for six months.

Hoisin Sauce

Fills 4–5 small (150ml/5fl oz) jars

300g/10½oz/2¼ cups onions, peeled and
  quartered
75g/2¾oz/½ cup garlic cloves, peeled
2–4 hot red chillies, roughly chopped
200g/7oz/¾ cup fresh root ginger, peeled
  and roughly chopped
1kg/2¼lb ripe plums, halved and stoned
100ml/3½fl oz/½ cup dark soy sauce
500ml/18fl oz/6¾ cups Japanese rice wine
  vinegar
6 star anise, finely ground
500g/18oz/2¾ cups caster (superfine) sugar

Home-made, this classic Chinese sauce is delicious and contains no MSG. I use it on all meats, and especially love it with shredded confit of duck served piled on a salad of bitter leaves. I like adding chillies but these are, naturally, optional.

Put the onions, garlic, chilli and ginger into a blender and whiz until you have a finely chopped mixture.

Place this mixture in a heavy pan and add the plum halves and the soy sauce and vinegar. Bring to the boil, cover, then simmer for about 20–30 minutes or until all the ingredients are very soft.

Rub the mixture through a fine sieve or use a mouli fitted with the finest blade. Put the purée back into the pan and add the star anise and the sugar. Return the mixture to the heat and simmer, stirring often until the sauce thickens. Pot the sauce into sterilized glass jars and cover in the usual way (see pages 165–6). Keeps for up to twelve months in a cold larder.

Sweet Chilli Sauce

Fills 1 medium (300ml/10fl oz) jar

10 garlic cloves, peeled
8 fresh red chillies, roughly chopped
10cm/4in fresh root ginger, peeled and
    roughly chopped
finely grated zest of 4 limes
1 bunch fresh coriander (cilantro)
150g/5½oz/¾ cup unrefined caster
    (superfine) sugar
250ml/9fl oz/1¼ cups rice wine vinegar
2 tablespoons each of Thai fish sauce and
    light soy sauce
1 teaspoon sesame oil

At Peter Gordon's restaurant they mix some of this sauce into soured cream to make a dressing for prawns. I love the combination as a dip served with corn chips.

This sauce is based on one I tried at The Sugar Club when that talented chef Peter Gordon cooked there. I love his food and was inspired to make a simpler version of his recipe.

Use with grilled shrimps, chicken and pork – in fact, almost any grilled foods!

Put the garlic, chillies, ginger, lime zest and coriander (cilantro), stalks and all, into a food processor and process until you have a fine purée.

Put the sugar and vinegar into a saucepan and cook over a low heat until the sugar dissolves. Turn up the heat and simmer until the mixture thickens, which will take about 5 minutes. Now stir in the spice paste, add the sauces and sesame oil, and boil for a further 2–3 minutes.

Pot into a sterilized jar and seal with a vinegar-proof lid (see pages 165–6). Store in a cold larder or the fridge for up to three months.

Marinades

Marinating meat, fish or vegetables is a good way of adding flavour and, with meat, tenderizing somewhat tougher cuts. From a simple mix of oil and chopped herbs to a more complex cooked marinade, if you have the time it's worth the effort.

I'm giving some marinades below, but once you get the hang of the technique you can make your own combination of flavours.

Do use good oil. I prefer extra virgin olive oil, apart from the oriental marinade, when groundnut or peanut oil is the right choice.

Vinegar and lemon juice 'cook' the meat or fish, so use judiciously.

Salt also changes the texture, as it can cause juices to leach out, so is usually added just before cooking.

Basting the meat/fish with the marinade as it cooks adds depth of flavour.

If you want to use leftover marinade again, or serve it as a sauce, it must be cooked as it will have come into contact with raw food. Pour leftover marinade into a saucepan and bring to the boil, making sure it boils for 2 minutes.

I marinate meat for several hours, often overnight. Fish and shellfish, on the other hand, need only a short time, say 30 minutes to an hour.

Simple Citrus Marinade

Fills 1 small (150ml/5fl oz) jar

1 shallot, peeled and finely chopped
2–3 tablespoons olive oil
1 garlic clove, peeled and crushed
finely grated zest and juice of 1 orange
  and 1 lemon
2 tablespoons chopped fresh coriander
  (cilantro)
freshly ground black pepper
a dash of Tabasco sauce
a spoonful of clear honey (optional)

Make a batch of this marinade and store in a bottle in the fridge ready for use. It's good as a marinade for chicken, pork or fish.

Cook the shallot in the oil until soft, about 5–7 minutes, then add the garlic and cook for a further 2 minutes. Now add the other ingredients and simmer for a final 2 minutes.

Remove from the heat and allow to cool before putting in a sterilized jar (see pages 165–6). Top with a lid, and store in the fridge for up to four weeks.

Rosemary, Honey & Cider Vinegar Marinade

Fills 1 small (150ml/5fl oz) jar

8 tablespoons olive oil
4 tablespoons cider vinegar
2 tablespoons runny honey
1–2 garlic cloves, peeled and crushed
sea salt and freshly ground black pepper
4 sprigs fresh rosemary, chopped

Oriental Marinade

Fills 1 small (150ml/5fl oz) jar

4 tablespoons sesame oil
4 garlic cloves, peeled and chopped
2 teaspoons finely chopped coriander
    (cilantro) root and stalks
2 small fresh red chillies, finely chopped
2 tablespoons fish sauce
4 tablespoons light soy sauce
4 tablespoons light vegetable oil
1 teaspoon raw palm or soft brown sugar

This is perfect for stir-fries of chicken or shrimps. Coriander stalk and root are much fuller in flavour than the leaves, so try to use them for this marinade, leaving the leaves to scatter on the cooked dish.

Mix all the ingredients together and simmer for 5 minutes before pouring into a sterilized glass jar and topping with a lid (see pages 165–6).

Store in the fridge for up to three weeks.

Rather a tasty one this, excellent for any white meat and rather tougher cuts of steak on the barbecue.

Mix the ingredients together in a small saucepan and simmer for 5 minutes.

Cool and pour into a sterilized glass jar (see pages 165–6). Top with a lid and store in the fridge until needed. It keeps for four weeks.

Flavoured Salts

I first started using flavoured salt when I wanted to serve some quails' eggs for a party. I knew celery salt was the usual dipper, but I had none. So I toasted some cumin seeds in a pan, added some coarse salt and whizzed the whole lot in a spice mill. The results exceeded my expectations.

These salts are an excellent accompaniment to fresh bread and an olive oil dip. Serve in small dishes alongside your pepper grinder.

Flavoured salts keep for months, but their flavour is best in the first six weeks. Store in a small clean jar in a cool dark cupboard.

Whole Spice Salt

Makes enough for 4 dippers

1 tablespoon whole spice (cumin or fennel seeds, pink peppercorns, chilli flakes etc.)
4 tablespoons coarse salt crystals

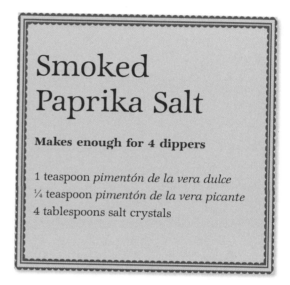

Smoked Paprika Salt

Makes enough for 4 dippers

1 teaspoon *pimentón de la vera dulce*
¼ teaspoon *pimentón de la vera picante*
4 tablespoons salt crystals

This recipe uses whole spices freshly ground. You can naturally use powdered spice to make your salts but, with the notable exception of smoked paprika salt, freshly ground is better.

Gently toast the spice in a dry pan until it smells nutty. Place the spice and salt in a spice mill and whiz until ground. Store in a screw-top jar.

You can use a variety of seeds to flavour your salts, but it's best to only use one spice at a time. Cumin is delicious with quails' eggs, sprinkled on hummus and seasoning cheese on toast. Fennel is excellent with anything fishy and with pâtés.

Pimentón de la vera *is one of my favourite ingredients. It's smoked Spanish paprika and has the most wonderful full, sweet, smoky flavour. It comes in two varieties,* dulce, *which is sweet, and* picante, *which is very hot indeed.*

Place the ingredients in a pestle and mortar and grind until fine.

Store in a screw-top jar.

Use with fish or chicken or almost anything; my new favourite is to sprinkle it on buttered popcorn.

Flavoured Sugars

A few jars of perfumed sugar allow you to jazz up all manner of dishes, from simple cinnamon toast to an exotic cardamom sugar sprinkle on rice pudding or yoghurt.

Here are two of my favourites but, applying the same principles, you will quickly be able to create your own. Flavoured sugars keep for many months but are best used within six weeks of making. Store in a cool dark cupboard or larder.

Each recipe makes about 115g/4oz.

Cinnamon Sugar

10cm/4in cinnamon stick
115g/4oz/½ cup caster (superfine) sugar

Whiz together in a spice mill, then store in a screw-top jar. Use on hot buttered toast, baked apples, waffles and pancakes.

Lavender Sugar

Lavender stalks
115g/4oz/½ cup caster (superfine) sugar

This is a wonderfully fragrant sugar – excellent when used in cakes and biscuits.

Pick lavender flowers when heavily scented and bury in the sugar.

Store in a screw-topped jar for 1 week before using. Other heavily scented edible flowers and herbs can also be used in this fashion.

Cardamom Sugar

1 tablespoon cardamom pods
115g/4oz/½ cup caster (superfine) sugar

Gently crush the pods to open them. Pick out the black seeds – you should have about 1 teaspoonful. Discard the pods.

Whiz the seeds and sugar together in a spice mill until finely ground. Store in a screw-top jar. Use on rice pudding, yoghurt or any other creamy treat, or in a chai latte (usually green tea with hot frothed milk).

AIR-DRYING

Introduction

Air-drying and Oven-drying

When it comes to preserving food, drying is one of the oldest processes known to man, and both wind and sun have been harnessed to achieve this aim from the earliest of times. Drying works so well because moisture is necessary for bacterial growth: no water, ergo no bacterial action, and your food can be safely stored until needed.

It is said that the Ancient Egyptians were the first to discover dried food – dates and figs that had fallen from trees became buried in hot sand and, when dug up, had been preserved. The sand dried and heated at the same time, thus killing bacteria, and this technique was developed by the Egyptians to include other fruits as well as small fish.

Mediterranean countries have always known the value of drying foods in the plentiful sun. Tomatoes are sun-dried throughout southern Italy and in Sicily a concentrated tomato paste is made by spreading puréed tomatoes on long tables in the open air. This paste is regularly turned throughout the intense August heat until the moisture evaporates and is a fraction of its initial volume. I once ate sun-dried ewe in Cyprus. It tastes much as you would expect, rather like chewy mutton, and I'm still hoping the small dark specks that covered the meat were indeed herbs and spices, as I was assured. Mushrooms, aubergines, courgettes (zucchini), beans, peaches, apricots and many other vegetables, pulses and fruit are all dried in the sun to store for winter.

Scandinavian countries, while less hot and sunny than those that surround the Mediterranean, have long utilized the brisk cold winds that blow around the coast in the summer months to good effect, drying stockfish in Sweden and Denmark, and *kuivaliha*, reindeer meat, in Finland. In North America, indigenous tribes as far apart as Texas and Alaska dried seal meat and buffalo, fish and berries to take with them on their migrations. Alpine countries air-dry beef as *bresaola* in Italy and *Bündnerfleisch* in Switzerland, while in China for centuries they have been wind-drying meat, especially sausages, and fish. Far Eastern food is often flavoured with dried fish, especially dried shrimp paste, a powerfully tasting ingredient, but one which, if used carefully, adds an extraordinary depth of flavour.

All of these foods were dried to preserve them, to make them easier to store and transport, and to guard against times of shortage. Indeed, many historians have said that, when man discovered how to dry and therefore store his food, he took the first steps towards civilization.

In this chapter, I am talking about food that is rendered as water-free as possible. Some foods are half-dried, having been heavily salted, and those are covered in Chapter 5.

Food Drying

This method of preserving is as old as time and used to depend on long dry autumns and large sheds with racks on which to place the prepared fruit and vegetables. If done on anything more than a small domestic scale, some sort of heat was necessary. In south-west France, plums are dried in wood-fired ovens to give the regional speciality, *pruneaux d'Agen* (prunes). While most of the plums are dried until well shrivelled, some are kept '*demi-cuit*', half cooked, ready to store in brandy and serve as dessert.

These days, dried fruits form an important part of our diets, and it seems as if each week a new wonder berry is announced: cranberries, blueberries and now goji berries (also known as wolfberries). All these berries, in common with most dried fruit, have high levels of antioxidants, which are unaffected by the drying process. Drying has the benefit of keeping many of the nutrients in food unchanged. Dried fruits are very rich in vitamins A and K, they are high in fibre, and contain natural sugars and fruit acids which contribute to our general and digestive health. And with a small packet of raisins containing the equivalent nutrients of the same number of whole grapes, they make the perfect easy-to-carry snack.

Removing moisture from food dramatically increases its keeping time and makes it less bulky to store. Ships' biscuits were baked until rock-like, then reconstituted once on board, allowing for a voyage's worth of food to be stored easily and not to impact on space needed for cargo or ammunition.

A small saddlebag stuffed with biltong and berries can give sufficient food for a long hunting trip. Today's soldiers take dehydrated rations into war zones to reduce the weight of their packs, and explorers everywhere know the value of space- and weight-saving when it comes to provisioning for their exploits.

The modern home is not quite as well equipped for drying as those of our forebears. We have, to the best of our abilities, eliminated draughts, warmed our houses with central heating and converted the outhouse into a home/work unit. Lines of salt cod drying in our gardens might look a little out of place amongst the daisies, and many of us do not have a handy apple store or even any space at all in our crowded homes.

For that reason, the following recipes are made using either your oven or one of the many commercially available dehydrators.

Air-drying

Air-drying is the simplest way to dry foods, and the most easily realized. Bunches of herbs can be tied with string and hung on hooks in breezy locations, perhaps the garden shed, a conservatory or a porch – anywhere sheltered from the elements with a good current of air. A sunny day with a light breeze will have herbs dried in no time when hung from the washing line.

I dry chillies and bay leaves by making a string of them using a needle and thread, then hanging them in my kitchen window. If you have a big stone fireplace you could copy our ancestors and hang the chillies adjacent to the chimney, where the combination of air and smoke will do the trick.

Mushrooms can be thinly sliced and laid on racks to dry in a warm dry room or, if protected from birds and insects, on tables in the sun. Porcini (cep) and field mushrooms work particularly well, and can be dried with no extra heat. Be canny about the weather, and don't attempt to try air-drying if a prolonged period of rain or humidity is forecast.

Oven-drying

Adapting traditional drying techniques to today's home needs a little thought. Being thrifty, I like to use residual heat in my oven for drying, but the downside to this option is you will have trays of semi-dried fruits hanging around until the next time the oven is hot. If that time is far off, the fruit will spoil before it dries.

Should you wish to use your oven for drying you will need to plan ahead. Most foods need to be dried for at least 6 hours, and therefore will be dried over several days. This method is obviously not suitable for drying meat.

The cool oven of a kitchen range such as an Aga can be used for drying purposes with good effect, and such use makes better sense of the continuous heat it gives out! The main issue with using an Aga for drying food is that the heavy doors seal in any moisture coming from the food, creating humidity inside the oven. Opening the door and turning the food frequently overcomes this problem. Those of us without Agas, though, can resort to buying small domestic dehydrators.

Drying in a Dehydrator

I first tried one of these machines when I had the urge to make biltong. I had recently returned from Cape Town, where I had enjoyed this high-protein and low-fat snack. Biltong is said to have been brought to Africa by Dutch settlers who cured, spiced and dried the meat to give a lightweight, easily transportable food. While the spicing may have come from Holland, the drying must surely, I think, pre-date Africa's colonization.

Biltong, like its American cousin, jerky, has a long and illustrious history. Both were once the traditional foods of cowboys and ranchers, but I think now make an excellent lunch-box alternative to pre-packed pepperoni salamis.

Dehydrators come in different sizes, with differing number of racks on which to dry; powered by electricity, they dry through a combination of heat and air. While there is an initial outlay, the dehydrator, once invested in, can be used for all your food drying and, with care, can be used to dry more than one food type at a time. If I'm drying fruit or meat, and have some space left, I cut some herbs from the garden and dry them on the top rack. I always stick to the rule that meat is placed under fruit and vegetables, never above.

Only the best-quality foods can be dried. It is a waste of effort to dry anything second-rate, so choose with care. As the drying process takes several hours, placing the dehydrator in another room saves you listening to the hum through the day. To ensure the food dries evenly you will need to take a little extra care. You must as far as possible cut the food into similar-sized pieces, and the thinner these pieces are the more rapidly they will dry. The individual pieces of food will need to be well spaced on the racks and they must be turned at least three or four times during the drying process. It is of the utmost importance that the foods are completely dry before storing them.

Storing Dried Foods

The important thing to bear in mind when storing dried fruits, herbs and vegetables is that the place you store them is dry. If the pantry or larder is damp, the food will quickly reabsorb the moisture you have so carefully got rid of, and spoil.

Fruits, vegetables and herbs can be stored in airtight tins or plastic boxes, and herbs in screw-topped glass jars. I wrap biltong and jerky in greaseproof (waxed) paper and store in the fridge. A dry cold room would be fine for storing both, but if there is any sign of spoiling when you come to use these meats, discard them.

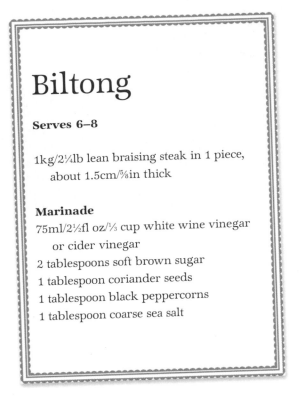

Biltong

Serves 6–8

1kg/2¼lb lean braising steak in 1 piece,
about 1.5cm/⅝in thick

Marinade
75ml/2½fl oz/⅓ cup white wine vinegar
or cider vinegar
2 tablespoons soft brown sugar
1 tablespoon coriander seeds
1 tablespoon black peppercorns
1 tablespoon coarse sea salt

Biltong hails from southern Africa. It is air-dried meat that has been spiced and salted before drying. I make my biltong with beef, but in Africa it is made with a variety of meats, often wild game. If you have access to venison, this recipe works well, and the girl who shared the recipe with me, Mel, who is from Kenya, regularly uses muntjac, which is delicious.

Originally meant as a convenience or fast food, biltong is high in protein and low in fat – if a little salty! I love it to chew on with a glass of chilled wine, and it's excellent as a snack on long car or train journeys.

Cut the meat into long slices about 4–5mm/¼in thick. You want to cut across the grain of the steak and make the pieces of biltong as long as possible.

Mix the marinade ingredients together in a china or glass dish, stirring to dissolve the sugar. Place the meat in the marinade, mix well to make sure all the meat is coated, then cover and chill for 12–24 hours. Lift the meat from the dish and pat the strips dry with kitchen paper (paper towels).

Place in a single layer on the tray of your dehydrator, and dry for 12 hours or until completely dry, turning once or twice.

Store the biltong in a dry covered container. I use the fridge, but if you have a cold larder, this would work well. Biltong keeps for six weeks.

✳ ✳ ✳ ✳ ✳ ✳ ✳ ✳ ✳ ✳ ✳ ✳ ✳ ✳ ✳ ✳ ✳ ✳ ✳ ✳

Beef Jerky

Serves 6–8

1kg/2¼lb lean braising steak in 1 piece,
about 1.5cm/⅝in thick

Rub
1 tablespoon soft brown sugar
1 tablespoon coarse sea salt
1 tablespoon sweet smoked paprika
1 teaspoon coarsely ground black pepper
⅛–¼ teaspoon hot smoked paprika

Beef jerky is the North American version of biltong, much favoured by early settlers and their Indian neighbours. It was eaten dry or added to bean stews when it needed very long cooking. I eat it as a snack much as you would salami. This air-dried meat differs from biltong (see page 234) as it has a dry rub rather than a wet marinade. I use a mixture of hot and sweet paprika as the main seasonings along with the ubiquitous salt and pepper, adding a little fresh thyme for extra pizzazz, but you can use whatever flavours you like. Star anise, dry ginger, cumin, fennel – there is a long list of potential candidates.

It almost goes without saying that the meat used for this recipe must be the freshest and the best. Ask your butcher to cut it for you if you like.

Cut the meat into strips or triangles no more than 5mm/¼in thick and about 10 x 30cm/4 x 12in.

Mix the ingredients for the rub together and then rub this on to the meat, making sure all sides are covered.

Place the meat in a single layer on the racks of a dehydrator and dry, turning the meat twice, for about 8–10 hours. The meat will have lost about 80% of its weight.

Store, wrapped in waxed paper in an airtight tin, in a cold larder or fridge for six weeks.

Drying Fruits & Vegetables

When you have a glut of fruit in the orchard, or come home carrying bags of apples and pears from visits to friends, you will wonder how to make the bounty last. Whilst I prefer to pickle or freeze fruits, there is a trend now towards drying them for storage, and this is most easily accomplished in a dehydrator.

Most fruit can be dried, including: apples, pears, bananas, cherries, strawberries, plums, mango and pineapple. Vegetables such as carrots, courgettes (zucchini), aubergines, red bell peppers, pumpkin, mushrooms, onions, peas and beans can all be dried successfully too.

To prepare the fruit or vegetable, cut it into thin slices, usually about 5mm/¼in thick. I core apples, but not pears. I peel carrots, but not courgettes and aubergines. Peas and beans can be placed on the trays of the dehydrator whole. I especially like to dry borlotti beans, which I grow in my garden, to store for use in winter soups.

Lay the fruit or vegetable slices on the racks provided in the dehydrator. Switch on, and dry until crisp; the time will vary with the fruit or vegetable used and the thickness of the slices. The handbook should give you approximate timings.

Once dry, store the fruit or vegetables in an airtight tin or wrap in waxed paper and place on a shelf in the pantry.

Tomatoes can be dried in the dehydrator in slices, but are better oven-dried, then stored in oil (see page 241).

Dried Herbs

You will get the best results when drying herbs if you use full-flavoured herbs to start with! I would love to recommend drying basil and coriander (cilantro), but dried they are a poor shadow of their fresh selves, and so I really feel they are not worth the effort. The same goes for chervil. Marjoram, thyme, tarragon and rosemary are excellent, however – they are hardy herbs – and mint also works well.

Pick the herbs when they are just beginning to mature, before any flowers open. The best time to gather your herbs is early morning after the dew has dried. Make sure they are clean. If necessary rinse in cold water and then pat dry with a cloth or kitchen paper (paper towels).

If using a dehydrator, lay the herbs in a single layer on the trays provided, and switch on. Run it until the herbs are very crisp and dry, about 4–6 hours.

If using the oven, I spread the herbs on baking sheets lined with clean newspaper or kitchen paper. Place these in your oven once you have finished cooking and the herbs will dry while the oven cools. You may have to repeat the drying over two or three days.

Once the herbs are dry, crumble them up and store in airtight jars, in a dark cupboard. The herbs will keep quite happily for twelve months, but will gradually lose their intensity over that time.

Mint Tea Bags

fresh mint leaves
muslin
needle and thread

If you have a prolific herb bed and love, as I do, to drink herbal teas, it is simplicity itself to make your own. Mint is the obvious one, but other herbs can be used. Fennel, sage and blackcurrant leaves all work well, and if you know anyone with a camomile lawn, what bliss!

Pick the mint leaves early in the morning, choosing bright mid-sized leaves. Try to make sure the leaves are clean when picked so the herbs will not need washing.

Pick the leaves from the stems, and dry as outlined above, either in the dehydrator, or in a cool oven. When the herbs are completely dry and crisp, crumble lightly into a bowl.

Cut the muslin into oblongs 16 x 8cm/ 6¼ x 3¼in, fold in half and sew up the two long sides. Put about 1–2 teaspoons dried mint into each bag and sew up the remaining side. An alternative is to cut 15cm/6in squares and tie the tops with cotton, making a loose pouch.

Store the bags in a jar or tin out of direct sunlight. They will keep for six months.

This is the perfect way to store a glut of really ripe tomatoes if you have an Aga or similar type of cooker. If you are using a conventional oven you may need to either run it on low for 6–8 hours or dry your tomatoes over a few days, using the residual heat whenever the oven is turned off.

I've tried all sizes of tomatoes and feel that the medium fleshy round or plum tomatoes dry best. Large ones take too long and cherry tomatoes have too big a skin-to-flesh ratio.

Whilst my recipe is for 1kg/2¼lb, do make more if your oven allows.

The first stage is to salt the tomatoes to remove as much juice as possible. You have to be fairly bold with the salt, remembering that it will add to the preservation of the fruit. Begin by cutting the tomatoes in half and laying them on a rack over a tray. Sprinkle on the salt and leave for 48 hours.

Preheat your oven to its very lowest, or follow as described above.

Place the tomatoes on a baking sheet, discarding any juices that have run from them. Sprinkle over the herbs and drizzle with 50ml/2fl oz of olive oil.

Dry in an oven until they are much shrunken in size and very chewy.

Pack the hot tomatoes into hot sterilized jars (see page 165), pressing down well. Pour on olive oil until the tomatoes are covered.

Cover and store in a cold larder or the fridge. Use within four weeks. If you see any signs of fermentation or mould, discard the contents of the jar.

Oven-dried Tomatoes

Makes approx. 400g/14oz

1kg/2¼lb ripe, fleshy, medium tomatoes
3–4 tablespoons coarse sea salt
1 teaspoon dried mixed herbs
olive oil

These tomatoes make an excellent part of an ante pasta plate when served with the marinated olives on page 202.

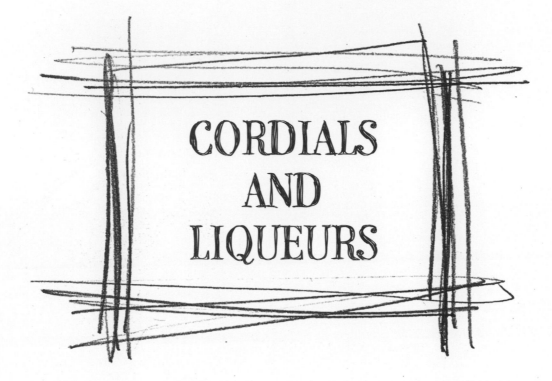

CORDIALS
AND
LIQUEURS

Introduction

I quite like the ambiguous nature of the word 'cordial', meaning as it does both being cheerful and friendly, and a sweet drink that is often alcoholic. I embrace both of these charming ideas, and whilst one may not always find being cheerful and friendly easy, cordials fortunately are simple to make. Who knows, a sip of the latter might lead to the former.

I tend to think of cordials as being non-alcoholic drinks like squash and lemonade. Some are quite as sophisticated as their boozy cousins, and make an excellent alternative to wine at parties and barbecues. Many non-alcoholic cordials can be used in making punches when they are diluted with white wine and sometimes given a kick of brandy, but for everyday use I dilute my cordials with cold water and plenty of ice. Fizzy water works well, and last winter I developed a taste for the pink grapefruit and ginger cordial (see page 254) made up with hot water. Very warming on a snowy day.

I serve the liqueurs after dinner, or sometimes in place of sherry before lunch. Diluted with chilled white wine, the liqueurs make excellent long drinks in the French manner.

Equipment

You need little special equipment but here, as always, everything does need to be spotlessly clean, and all storage bottles should be sterilized before use. The easiest way to do this is to wash them well with hot soapy water, rinse with clean water and then submerge them in water with sterilizing tablets – the sort sold to sterilize babies' bottles. These are widely available from chemists and supermarkets.

You can buy very lovely glass bottles with corks or hinged wire stoppers. These make your cordials into attractive gifts. For home use, I keep the bottle of the spirit that I used in the recipe. For frozen spirits, I use a screw-topped glass bottle. Do take care when freezing liquids as they need to have a high alcohol content in order to only become gelid when frozen. Low alcohol liquids freeze solid and expand and the bottle may shatter. Anyone who has put a bottle of wine in the freezer to give it a quick chill and then forgotten about it can attest to this. Although, if you leave space for headroom, in a screw-topped bottle, low-alcohol drinks could freeze successfully.

When straining your cordials, use a clean muslin cloth that has been scalded with boiling water.

China or glass bowls and metal spoons are best, as wooden spoons can harbour spores and bacteria.

Ingredients

The lovely thing about making these drinks is that you need very few exotic ingredients, and once you have the knack the world is your cordial. I've made delicious kumquat and passionfruit brandy as well as rhubarb gin, and both were excellent.

Alcohol

Many of the following recipes call for alcohol. I use vodka as a base spirit as it has little discernible flavour of its own and so readily takes to being made into liqueurs. Gin is a spirit that has been infused with a variety of aromatics during the distillation process, so will add complexities to any drink it is used for. I find gin is excellent with stone fruit like damsons and sloes, but conversely I love raspberry gin, too.

Brandy is best used for strongly aromatic drinks – oranges and peaches work well, but not soft fruit like strawberries. I recently tasted sloe whisky and was pleasantly surprised at how delicious it was. I've not made it myself, but would use a recipe based on the damson gin on page 251, substituting the necessary ingredients.

European countries sell alcohol for fruit liqueur-making that I buy if I'm travelling by car, as this works very well when making liqueurs at home. It is pure alcohol, of about 40% proof. This level of alcohol is the best to use as it gives the best flavour. Cheaper supermarket own-brands will often only be 35–37.5% proof, but will still work well.

Fruit

A great many fruits are suitable for making into liqueurs, primarily fruit with a distinct flavour. All fruits should be of the finest quality, ripe and without blemish. Frozen fruit, apart from strawberries, work especially well, as the fruit is already partially broken down by the freezing process.

Damsons, sloes and other small members of the plum family make good liqueurs – their sour flavour and deep colour add complexity to the drink. These cordials are best left for at least one year to mature, if you can wait that long.

Many soft fruit can be used in cordial-making, and these give up their flavour quite quickly. Strawberries and raspberries are the quickest, and a good flavour can be extracted from them in a matter of a few days.

Blackcurrants are used in making that wonderful French drink, Cassis, often added to chilled white wine for Kir, or champagne for Kir Royale. Cranberries, another sour dense berry, should be roughly chopped before use to speed up the steeping process. Cranberry vodka makes a wonderfully festive Christmas drink that looks beautiful served in tiny liqueur glasses. Both Cassis and cranberry

vodka can be made using the instructions for blueberry vodka on page 250, adjusting the quantity of sugar to taste.

Citrus fruit is the base of many cordials. Make these when the fruit is at its best early in the year, and, again, make the cordial promptly once you've bought the fruit. Oranges, lemons, limes and grapefruit are all waxed to prolong their shelf life, but the fresher the better is the rule. Scrub all citrus under hot running water unless it is marked un-waxed.

Limoncello, that wonderfully fragrant drink that hails from southern Italy, is a delight to make at home. The zest of half a dozen lemons is finely grated into a bottle of vodka, and left for six weeks for the essential oils to transfer into the alcohol. Sugar is then added to taste and the liqueur strained and bottled. Limoncello is usually served chilled, so bear this in mind when you are adding the sugar. Any drink served very cold or iced must be unpalatably sweet at room temperature to taste right when frozen.

Aromatics

Many interesting spice combinations can be used in making cordials and I find them especially useful in non-alcoholic drinks where they add complexity. Star anise, cinnamon, ginger (both fresh and powdered), cardamom and even coriander seeds work well, either separately or in combination.

And don't forget chillies. Chilli vodka, stored in the freezer, makes wonderful Martinis and Bloody Marys. Chilli vodka is the simplest to make. Fresh chillies are roughly chopped and placed in the bottle with the spirit. This is left to steep for a week and then is ready to use. If you feel there is sufficient heat in the vodka, strain out the chillies. No sugar is added to chilli vodka...

Sugar

For clarity of the finished liqueur or cordial I like to use white sugar, either caster (superfine) or granulated as takes your fancy.

Sometimes stock syrup is called for when making mixed drinks. This is easily made using a simple recipe that takes one measure of water heated with an equal measure of white sugar until the sugar dissolves and then boiled rapidly until the syrup thickens (about 5 minutes for 300ml/10fl oz/¼ cups water).

Pomegranate Molasses

Makes approx. 600ml/1 pint

500ml/18fl oz/2¼ cups fresh pomegranate
juice (approx. 2kg/4½lb whole ripe
pomegranates)
400g/14oz/2 cups white sugar
1 teaspoon lemon juice

This is a Middle Eastern staple, and a wonderful addition to any larder. I use this sweet-sour syrup drizzled over roasted vegetables, and I put a dash in dressings for tabbouleh and other grain salads. It's delicious on pancakes and sublime with a rich rice pudding.

You must use the juice from actual pomegranates, not the sort you get in the chill cabinet. I find Middle Eastern markets or street markets are the best place to buy pomegranates in this quantity.

Cut the pomegranates in half and squeeze out the juice. I think the best way to do this is using an orange juicer. If you have an electric one, so much the better. If not, then you can use a citrus reamer.

Strain the juice through scalded muslin and then put in a pan over a moderate heat. Add the sugar and lemon juice, and stir gently until the sugar has dissolved, then turn up the heat and bring the liquid to the boil.

Cook over a high heat until the liquid has become thick and syrupy, about 7–10 minutes.

Cool a little, then pour into sterilized bottles or jars (see page 165). Store in a cold dark pantry or the fridge for six months.

Try this syrup on chilled Greek-style yogurt for breakfast. Sublime.

✳ ✳

Strawberry Cocktail Vodka

Makes approx. 750ml/26fl oz

400g/14oz/3¼ cups ripe strawberries
60g/2¼oz/⅓ cup caster (superfine) sugar
500ml/18fl oz/2¼ cups vodka (40% proof
   is best)

*Flavoured vodkas make the most
wonderful cocktails, and this strawberry
vodka is no exception. I love to drink this
either iced from the freezer or mixed with
Champagne. It is delicious poured over
ice-cream and added to custards for very
special trifles.*

*Make this when strawberries are at
their most full-flavoured and store for
three months before use... if you can!*

In a glass bowl or jug, mash the hulled
strawberries with the sugar. Pour over
the vodka and mix well. (Keep the bottle.)

   Cover the jug or bowl with a double
layer of clingfilm (plastic wrap) and leave
in a dark place for two to three months.

   Strain through scalded muslin and then
pour into the clean reserved vodka bottle.
Store in a cool dark place – it lasts for ever –
and freeze before serving.

This is a great hit on my book club
evenings mixed with chilled cava.
After a couple of glasses you could
even write your own novel...

Blueberry Vodka

Makes 750ml/26fl oz

450g/1lb/4½ cups blueberries
115g/4oz/½ cup caster (superfine) sugar
750ml/26fl oz/3¼ cups vodka (40% proof
   is best)

Make this lovely drink in late summer when blueberries are plentiful and sweet and serve it, ice cold, in tiny liqueur glasses after lunch or dinner. The colour is wonderful and blueberries are full of antioxidants and vitamin C. I've no idea whether any or all of the beneficial qualities withstand the steeping process, but we can hope that, finally, here is a drink that is good for you!

Don't forget to save the vodka bottle and its screw-top lid as you will need them later. As this vodka makes a lovely gift, you could buy pretty bottles with hinged rubber sealed lids and use these.

Place the blueberries and sugar in the goblet of a food processor or blender and whiz until the berries are finely chopped.

Transfer the mixture to a glass or china bowl and pour over the vodka. Stir and cover with a double layer of clingfilm (plastic wrap). Leave the bowl in a cool, dark place for three to four weeks.

Strain the mixture through scalded muslin and pour it into the saved vodka bottle. Screw on the lid and store in the freezer until needed. It will last indefinitely.

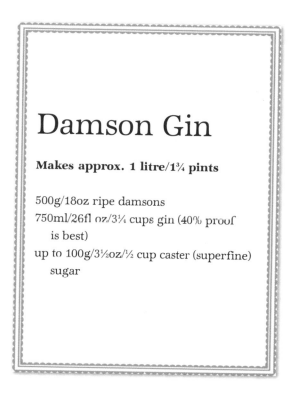

Damson Gin

Makes approx. 1 litre/1¾ pints

500g/18oz ripe damsons
750ml/26fl oz/3¼ cups gin (40% proof
   is best)
up to 100g/3½oz/½ cup caster (superfine)
   sugar

This gin is a relative of her wilder cousin, sloe gin. Damsons are available to even the most inner-city cook courtesy of autumn farmers' markets. If you own a damson tree, so much the better!

I find that putting the damsons in the freezer overnight helps the skins to break down faster, adding colour and flavour to the finished liqueur.

When you are ready to make the gin you have two options, both of which require that you thaw the fruit first. Now either prick the damsons with a silver fork, or put them into the goblet of a food processor, pressing the pulse button once or twice. I choose the latter, but have friends who swear only hand-pricking each damson makes the best gin.

Place the prepared damsons into a large china or glass bowl, pour on the gin, and stir in the sugar. Cover the bowl with two to three layers of clingfilm (plastic wrap) and put it in a cold dark place for two to three months. Reserve the gin bottles for later.

Strain the gin through a double layer of scalded muslin and pour into the reserved bottles. Now label and date and leave the gin to mature, again in a cool dark place, for as long as you are able. One year is good, three years better!

Wild Blackberry Gin

Makes approx. 750ml/26fl oz

450g/1lb/3 cups brambles/blackberries
225g/8oz/scant ¼ cups caster (superfine)
   sugar
700ml/1¼ pints/2½ cups gin (40% is best)

Put the blackberries into a pan with the sugar and heat gently until the sugar melts. Allow this mixture to cool. Then transfer it into a glass bowl or jug and pour over the gin. Stir and cover with clingfilm (plastic wrap), sealing tightly.

Shake or stir the mixture every other day for about a week, then leave to infuse for four to six weeks.

Strain through scalded muslin and replace in the reserved, clean screw-topped bottle. This keeps for at least a year.

Wild blackberries work perfectly here. They are rather bitter and complex in flavour and often too small to enjoy as fruit. As a liqueur, both these qualities become virtues.

Pink Grapefruit & Ginger Cordial

Makes approx. 1 litre/1¾ pints

800g/1¾lb/6 cups caster (superfine) sugar
450ml/16fl oz/2 cups water
200g/7oz/¾ cup fresh root ginger
3 pink grapefruit
55g/2oz citric acid

Home-made cordials are a real addition to your store-cupboard. Make them in small quantities and use within three months. I'm using pink grapefruit here but double the quantity of limes would work as well. A dash of chilli would add a certain zing and make this a base for a rather interesting cocktail.

Make a syrup by dissolving the sugar in the water and boiling for 5 minutes.

Meanwhile, whiz the ginger in a blender or food processor until finely chopped. Grate the zest from the grapefruit and squeeze out the juice.

Mix the zest, juice and ginger in a spotlessly clean glass bowl and pour over the hot syrup. Stir in the citric acid and cover with clingfilm (plastic wrap). Place in a cool dark room for four days, stirring each day with a clean metal spoon.

Strain through scalded muslin and pour into sterilized glass bottles (see page 165). Top with stoppers and store in a pantry for up to six months.

Christmas Punch Cordial

Makes approx. 750ml/26fl oz

225g/8oz/scant 1¼ cups white granulated
  sugar
600ml/1 pint/2 cups water
10cm/4in cinnamon stick, broken into
  pieces
2 teaspoons cardamom pods, crushed
1 teaspoon cloves, crushed
5cm/2in fresh root ginger, crushed
thinly peeled zest of 2 lemons and
  2 oranges, plus their juice

*You don't really need to keep this delicious
cordial for Christmas (as the base to a
fruity mulled red wine punch, perhaps),
as it makes a refreshing summer cooler
when mixed with fizzy water or chilled
white wine.*

First, make the sugar syrup by dissolving
the sugar in the water in a small saucepan.
Heat gently, and once the sugar has
completely dissolved, bring the syrup to
the boil and simmer for 5 minutes. Add the
spices, juices and zests and return the pan
to the boil for 60 seconds.

Remove from the heat and pour into a
spotlessly clean glass jug. Cover and leave
for 24 hours.

Strain the cordial through scalded
muslin into a clean jug and then store in
sterilized bottles (see page 165). Seal and
label, then store in a cool, dark place for
up to six months.

Elderflower Cordial

Makes approx. 3 litres/5¼ pints

1kg/2¼lb/5⅓ cups white sugar
1.8 litres/3¼ pints/6½ cups water
2 unwaxed lemons
2 well-scrubbed or unwaxed oranges
approx. 20 large elderflower heads
55g/2oz citric acid

Whilst this is a drink you can only make during a very few weeks in the year, it is one of the most evocative cordials. It is so easy to make and so delicious in summer drinks, fruit salads, sorbets and jellies. Combine it with gooseberry juice and gin for a deceptively mild-tasting cocktail.

Store the cordial in a cool dark place and do be sure to use spotlessly clean bottles: any residual beer or cider in your bottles and the cordial will ferment and the bottles explode!

Pick elderflowers first thing in the morning, shaking gently to remove any wildlife.

Make a syrup by dissolving the sugar in the water and boiling for 5 minutes.

Chop the whole fruit into 2.5cm/1in cubes and place with the dry flower heads in a large spotlessly clean glass or china bowl. Pour over the syrup, stir in the citric acid, and cover with a clean cloth.

Leave the bowl in a dark cool place for four days, stirring each day with a clean spoon.

Strain the syrup through scalded muslin and pour into sterilized bottles (see page 165). Store either in a cold larder or in the fridge for six months.

What's In My Larder?

❖ Pasta and Noodles

Pasta: tagliatelli, spaghetti, linguine, penne, pappardelle, farfalle, fusilli, rigatone
Small pasta for soups
Lasagne sheets
Thai rice noodles
Chinese rice noodles
Japanese soba noodles

❖ Grains

Bulgar wheat
Couscous
Polenta (yellow cornmeal)
Quinoa
Rice: basmati, Thai, wild rice, long-grain, arborio or vialone nano risotto rice, Valencia rice, pudding rice

❖ Beans and Other Pulses

Chickpeas
Borlotti beans
Cannellini beans
Butter beans
Red kidney beans
Green or Puy lentils

❖ Flours

Plain (all-purpose) white flour
Wholemeal (whole-wheat) flour
Granary flour
A wheat- or gluten-free flour
Cornflour (cornstarch)
Polenta

❖ Sugars

Caster (superfine) sugar (white and golden)
Granulated sugar (white and golden)
Light brown unrefined muscovado sugar
Dark brown unrefined muscovado sugar
Icing (confectioners') sugar
Unrefined white sugar
Molasses
Golden syrup

❖ Biscuits and Crackers

Amaretti (macaroons)
Gingernut biscuits
Sponge fingers
Rich tea and digestives
Water biscuits and crackers for cheese
Tortillas
Poppadums
Corn chips

❖ Cereals, Seeds and Nuts

Jumbo oats
Pinhead oatmeal
Linseeds
Sunflower seeds
Pumpkin seeds
Sesame seeds
Poppy seeds

❖ Dried Vegetables and Fruits

Sun-dried tomatoes
Dried chillies
Prunes
Dried apricots
Dried dates, stoned
Raisins/sultanas (golden raisins)

❖ Jars

Sun-dried tomatoes in olive oil
Artichoke hearts
Grilled vegetables in olive oil
Sauces (porcini, aubergine, pesto)
Fruits in syrup or brandy (cherries, peaches, apricots)

Tomato passata
A couple of jars of good, ready-made
    spaghetti sauce
Good mayonnaise
Mustards (Dijon, English and wholegrain
    and dry mustard powder)
Anchovies in oil (some in jars are salted, so
    need to be rinsed)
Capers, both small and the large caper
    berries
Cornichons or small gherkins
Fermented black beans

❖ Tins
Beans (cannellini, chickpeas, red kidney
    beans, baked beans)
Italian tomatoes (whole peeled, chopped)
Tomato purée
Beef consommé
Coconut milk and coconut cream
Tinned pineapple and tinned peaches
Condensed milk
Goose fat

❖ Fish
Sardines, French or Spanish, in olive oil
Tuna, Spanish or Italian, in olive oil
Mackerel fillets in oil
Anchovies in oil

❖ Sauces
Tabasco and/or other chilli sauces
Thai fish sauce
Japanese soy sauce (light, dark and
    wheat-free)
Liquid stock concentrate (chicken and
    vegetable)
Worcestershire sauce
Anchovy sauce
Mushroom ketchup
Tomato ketchup
Sweet chilli dipping sauce
Hoisin sauce

❖ Oils
Extra virgin olive oil (for cooking)
    and estate-bottled extra virgin olive
    oil (for dressing)
A light-tasting oil, I favour groundnut
Sesame oil

❖ Vinegars
Red and white wine vinegars
Rice wine vinegar
Cider vinegar
Distilled malt vinegar
Aged balsamic vinegar, a real Italian one,
    aged about 8 years

❖ Salt and Pepper
Coarse rock salt
Fine sea salt
Maldon salt or other coarse sea salt
Whole black/white peppercorns
Dried green peppercorns
Green peppercorns in brine

❖ Spices
A good selection of whole spices:
    cumin, coriander, cardamom,
    caraway, fennel, celery and mustard
    seeds, cinnamon sticks, cloves,
    juniper berries, star anise
A select few of ground spices: celery salt,
    powdered garlic, *pimentón de
    la vera*, *dulce* and *picante*

❖ Pickles and Jams
Redcurrant jelly
A good clear honey
A couple of jars of preserves or jams
Pickled onions
Pickled walnuts
Mint jelly
Horseradish sauce

Index

Acknowledgements

Any book is the work of many more people than the author, so thanks are due.

Firstly to Emily Preece-Morrison, who approached me with her idea and allowed me to run with it. And thank you too to Anova Books – I'm delighted to be being published by you.

Anna Cheifetz and Becca Spry both helped the book on its way. Martine Carter, my agent, kept a watchful eye on me.

I want to thank Richard Emson for teaching me how to make sausages at his wonderful butchers' shop, Salter's on Aldeburgh High Street.

The photographs perfectly set the mood of this book – thank you Diana – they are truly beautiful.

Thanks too to Joy Skipper who prepared all the food for the photography and was so complimentary about the dishes, even though she's not a meat eater!

Always thanks must go to my husband Bob, who defines the words 'long suffering' and copes stoically with a bad tempered wife and mountains of washing up.

I have an enthusiastic band of consumers in my daughters Jade and Amber and now, coming along quite well in the gastronomy stakes, my son-in-law Pete. Thanks for all the tasting and for knowing when not to comment adversely.

My mother helped enormously by recalling dishes she had grown up with, in the days when larders and meat safes were the norm.

My final and most heartfelt thank you must go to my editor and good friend Susan Fleming. She is, quite simply, the best.